S0-ADT-710

What leaders are saying about *The Shaking of the Nations...*

Dr. Daniel J. Griffiths is a seasoned leader and brilliant strategist with tremendous insight into the growth of the church. *The Shaking of the Nations* presents a powerful case for a triumphant church that seizes the coming harvest God is about to bring. It will challenge your thinking, build your faith, and prepare you for the exciting future that is ahead. I highly recommend it.

Ken Foreman, *Senior Pastor, Cathedral of Faith, San Jose, CA*

When I read Dan Griffiths' new book *The Shaking of the Nations,* his clear and well-documented presentation caused great excitement to well up in me. He challenges the "spiritual fatalism" in today's church with the ringing cry, "Get ready for the harvest!" — undergirding it with solid scriptural support. The "divine audacity" he presents is a compelling, exciting message for anyone serious about the near future, and should spark an "audacious" attitude in any Christian reader!

Ernest Gentile, *Co-Pastor, Church On The Hill, Ft. Sumner, NM*
Author of Awaken the Dawn, *and other books.*

Dr. Daniel Griffiths has located the kingdom pulse in his book *The Shaking of the Nations,* which details the final move of the Spirit before the Lord's return. It is such a "must read" for those who anticipate Jesus' glorious return that Northern California Bible College is working the book into the heart of its curriculum. We live on the cusp of the greatest moving of the Spirit since Pentecost -- and Dr. Griffiths explains why!

David Sell, *Dean, Northern California Bible College*

The Shaking of the Nations

Book 1 in *The Last Shaking* Series

by

Daniel J. Griffiths, D.Min.

The Shaking of the Nations
Copyright © 2015 Daniel J. Griffiths, D.Min
ARK Ministries International

All rights reserved. No part of this book may be reproduced, stored in a retrieval system, or transmitted in any form or by any means – electronic, mechanical, photocopying, recording, or otherwise – without the prior written permission of the publisher and the copyright owner. The only exception is brief quotations in printed reviews.

7710-T Cherry Park Dr, Ste 224
Houston, TX 77095
713-766-4272

The views expressed in this book are those of the author, and do not necessarily reflect those of the publisher.

Published in the United States of America.

eBook: 978-1-60796-870-2

Softcover: 978-0692526200

Hardcover: 978-1-60796-871-9

Dedication

I would like to dedicate this book to Karen, my wife of 46 years, who has been so gracious, loving, and patient with me. Even during the times I neglected her while I was wrapped up in writing, her support never wavered.

Every book is in fact a product of many hands, and is influenced by many minds. During the years *The Last Shaking* series was being birthed, dozens of friends and colleagues gave me valuable input, often after taking time to carefully read through early drafts. I am deeply grateful to them all.

I want to thank my editor, Jim Hatlo, for his tireless efforts. Without his help this book would not have happened. I want to thank my publisher, Eddie Smith, for his patient encouragement and wise suggestions.

Above all, I want to thank the Lord who kept his word to me, given way back during the Jesus Movement, that I would see and participate in the greater move of God that is beginning to happen.

The best is yet to come.

Table of Contents

God is going to shake the nations, awakening them to the precariousness of life in this world. Multitudes will seek stability and hope in Christ. God's leaders must build an expectant faith in the church to seize the amazing harvest opportunities that are coming.

PART ONE

God has called me to challenge a defeatist paradigm about the future of the church. Contrary to widespread pessimism, its most fruitful days lie ahead. We must awaken to what scripture and the spirit clearly teach: For those with courageous faith, the best is yet to come.

Chapter One

God is raising up prophetic voices to call the church to renewal for the great climactic harvest. When He called me, he gave me two key objectives to help the church prepare.

Chapter Two

The Promised Shaking

Over three thousand years ago God first prophesied a confrontation between his Kingdom and a fallen heaven and earth. That confrontation is at hand.

Chapter Three

The Shaking of the Earth

The coming divine shaking will be divided into two parts – the first being the literal shaking of the earth. Today's church is unprepared for this cataclysm.

Chapter Four

The Shaking of the Heavens

God also will shake the spiritual forces of the heavens. Through Jesus Christ, Satan has been displaced. From the church's heavenly position, it can take part in both the shaking of Satan's kingdom and the nations – provided that it is prepared.

PART TWO

The Great Harvest

The last two millennia have been an age of harvest. That age is drawing to an end – and a climactic wave is building that will sweep whole people groups into the Kingdom of God.

Chapter Five

The Age of Harvest

Jesus' keenest focus was on "fishing for men": harvesting people into the Kingdom. Jesus built his life and that of his church around the spiritual harvest.

Chapter Six

Preparing for the Harvest Wave

Has the church been succeeding in reaching every nation with the gospel? Yes – but it is sadly unready to disciple the astonishing harvest that God is ripening in the world today.

Chapter Seven

The Continuous Harvest

God prophesied a paradox – simultaneous sowing and reaping. Yet that is exactly what is coming at the end of this age.

Chapter Eight

The Jewish Harvest

The days are numbered for the gentile church to carry the full load of world evangelism. The first fruits of Israel will soon partner with the gentile church to bring in the great harvest.

Chapter Twelve

Building Audacious Faith

If God is becoming more and more audacious in his Kingdom witness, then as his people we must develop an audacious faith so he can greatly use us.

Chapter Thirteen

It's Later Than You Think

Jesus commanded the church to teach the "signs" of his coming, so God's people could live victorious lives at the end of this age. But who is listening?

Conclusion

A Net-breaking Harvest

An unimaginably vast harvest lies ahead. But God will only use harvesters who have made themselves ready.

APPENDIX I

APPENDIX II

APPENDIX III

The Call to Readiness

Readiness means a right relationship to God and a knowledge of where we are at present....

Readiness for God means that we are ready to do the tiniest little thing or the great big thing, it makes no difference....

And we are ready for it with all the alertness of our love for him.

A ready person never needs to get ready. Think of the time we waste trying to get ready when God has called.

Oswald Chambers
His Utmost for His Highest

www.utmost.org

Foreword

The Shaking of the Nations is a truly significant book for me. You see, my entire spiritual life and ministry is a result of a powerful shaking that can only be described as a true revival.

It was in the early 1970s when the Holy Spirit was being poured out on a generation of lost and confused young people. They were coming to Christ by the tens of thousands in California and in other places. Disillusioned with a broken culture and still desperately empty despite the promise of sex, drugs, and rock and roll, they were discovering life, healing, and reality in Jesus Christ.

Suddenly, many traditional churches were being flooded with hippies and hungry teenagers. Tens of thousands were baptized in the ocean waters at California beaches. Multitudes were filled with the Holy Spirit and experienced the genuine power of God in worship, prayer, spiritual gifts, and unusual miracles. Fresh songs were written that forever changed the church's way of doing worship. Countless families were changed and new ministries sprang up everywhere.

This revival intensified for nearly a decade, becoming well known as the "Jesus-People Movement." I was one of many who were profoundly transformed during that time.

Another young man touched by this movement was Daniel J. Griffiths. Dan and I met and became true friends years later in San Jose as fellow pastors, but we had common roots in the same revival. We've worked together for the best part of two decades to see churches unite in prayer and ministry to our community. We've labored and believed for transforming revival, engaging with some of the most incredible leaders in the church, government, and marketplace in our region. Together, we've laughed, cried, prayed, and prophesied many times, and I'm so grateful that to this day we're still connected in ministry.

Those early days of spiritual outpouring produced an amazing harvest. In my own life, for the past 35 years, I've served one church that was transformed by the Jesus People movement. It was in that church that I was married, trained, and ordained into the ministry. Our children and grandchildren are now growing into their futures within the same church.

I've seen many lives touched; I've written books and articles, trained thousands of international leaders, planted churches and spoken around the world. Everything God has done in my life was birthed in the shaking that came in the 1970s.

But like Dan Griffiths, I've never stopped looking for the next great move of God.

In this important book, Dr. Griffiths will guide you through some of the most inspiring Scriptures and timely principles you'll ever read. You'll understand with greater clarity God's plan for your present and your future. You'll discover what you must do to connect with Heaven's purpose in this generation. And you'll find yourself growing excited about the future of the church and the next revival that God has planned.

Forget the doomsday prophets, the naysayers, and the ivory-tower critics. Listen to Dan, and get ready for something supernatural to take shape in your world.

Now is the time for a book like this and Dan is just the person to write it. He is a trained theologian and a seasoned practitioner of the principles he champions. He's also witnessed the shaking of a generation.

But beyond that, Dan is a very credible prophet to the church. I've heard the Lord speak through Him many times. He is a welcome voice in my life. And as you read what God has shown Dan in *The Shaking of the Nations*, you'll no doubt be hearing God's voice in your life as well.

Dr. David Cannistraci
Lead Pastor, GateWay City Church, San Jose, CA
Author of *Apostles and the Emerging Apostolic Movement*

Introduction

As I listened to the news commentator reporting on terrorist activities in the Middle East, I was again impressed with how dangerous the world is becoming.

The commentator was interviewing the head of Homeland Security, who declared that his department was now tracking the "radicalization" of potential terrorists through all 50 states in the U.S.

He went on to say that it was not "if, but when" these radicalized home-grown terrorists would strike -- sowing fear and confusion into our nation.

Web-savvy terrorists are reaching out to unstable, alienated youth who are looking for a cause to give their lives meaning. Many are finding that cause in political and religious hatred. Such virtual recruiting is another addition to the list of menaces, human and natural, increasingly shaking the lives of people around the globe.

Over 15 years ago the Lord began speaking to me about becoming a prophetic voice to awaken the church to a coming climactic harvest – one that would be shaped by the last shaking God will bring to the nations. He would expose the myth of utopian peace in which so many have placed their hopes, and force mankind to see where our evil, rebellious hearts have taken us.

God is ready to let governments fall, financial institutions fail, and social unrest to mushroom – leaving people's lives so torn and shaken that they will be desperate to find something unshakable in this life.

This will herald the greatest harvest in church history.

But here is the great problem: The church is sadly unprepared. Were God to release tomorrow the full harvest wave he is building, it would overwhelm the church.

The signs are everywhere – and Jesus commanded his church to "stay awake and be alert," so that we wouldn't be surprised by the coming tumult. It is time to awaken, to sound the alarm.

But how can the church prepare for what it does not expect? How can believers find faith in what they have not been taught?

We must instill a fearless expectation in God's people: The Church is destined to become the mightiest force on earth in the last days. Yet, this vital paradigm is absent in the thinking of many Christian leaders. I pray that this book will be a powerful wake-up call for leaders who will believe, and will stride into the fields of the incredible harvest.

PART ONE

A Paradigm of Courage

I don't know how many times in my 42 years of pastoring I heard a church member relate some terrible event and then close by saying, "Well we really are in the last days, aren't we, pastor?"

This attitude pervades the thinking of both church leaders and church members. I call it "spiritual fatalism" -- the view that the world is only going to get worse, we are helpless to change it, and we might as well resign ourselves to the inevitable.

Oh, Christians will say that "we win" when Jesus comes again and the church is raptured. But too many have the idea that, up to that point, the church will increasingly be attacked, with believers simply holding on by their fingernails until Jesus comes. It's a dismal picture – so we shouldn't be surprised that most believers try not to think much about it.

As church leaders, we must take responsibility for the persistence of this fatalism. It arises from our preaching and teaching – and from our failure to accurately understand God's word.

It keeps the church earthbound when it could be "spiritually flying."

One of the greatest breakthroughs in aerodynamics was the discovery that an airplane's wings must be curved on top and flat on the bottom. The reason is that it takes longer for air to flow over the top of a curved wing than it does to pass under the flat underside of the wing. This design creates lift. The differences in air pressure keep the plane airborne.

Scripture is clear that God is ready to empower the church as never before. But for the wind of the Holy Spirit to give lift to the church, we need the right spiritual aerodynamics.

Faith in God's promises forms the wings of the church. Yet, as the church looks out at the world and ahead toward its future, fear and unbelief are robbing it of the ability to fly.

Jesus intended his church to live supernaturally when he sent the Holy Spirit at Pentecost. The church's witness, its strength, and its endurance, are rooted in "grace" - the Spirit-given ability to live above our earthly circumstances. But without faith and confidence in God's plans, our spiritual wings are clipped and our witness of the truth in Christ is greatly limited.

This is the challenge of this book: to replace the paradigm of spiritual fatalism with one of courage and Spirit-filled anticipation. The enormous challenges the church will face pale in contrast to the extraordinary opportunities and victories God has in store for it.

Some of the greatest heroes of the faith are about to step onto the stage of church history. But for that to fully happen, we must achieve a paradigm shift in church leadership and in the church as a whole. Changing our faith dynamics will release the church to soar on the wind of the Holy Spirit.

I pray that as you read this book you will develop an expectant and a courageous faith that God can use in the coming days.

CHAPTER ONE

The Calling

The year was 1971. I had been married less than two years. I was pastoring a small Baptist church when God used two converted hippies to draw me into the now-famous "Jesus Movement": a magnet for young drop-outs from American culture in the '60s and '70s.

At first I had no idea what I had gotten myself into -- but I saw hundreds of young people saved and brought into the Kingdom of God. It was exhilarating. When the Jesus Movement drew to an end, I sat in my church office wondering if I would ever experience anything like it again in my ministry.

Revivals like the Jesus Movement tend to spoil you, leaving you unwilling to settle for "church as usual." True revival makes you hungry for more of the pulsing presence and power of God's Kingdom as the Spirit does his incredible work.

As I sat at my desk, the Lord made me a promise: He said I would see a much greater move of his Spirit later in my life. For more than 40 years, I have held on to that promise.

God also assured me that I would be a "spiritual father" in the next move. That might seem strange and out of context, but I knew exactly what he meant. The impact of the Jesus Movement had been diluted through its early rejection by much of the American church. Left largely on their own, the Jesus kids had a dearth of spiritual fathers to give them guidance.

Long hair, torn blue jeans, granny dresses, and bare feet were typical of the converted hippies. Dressed that way, they were offensive to many mainstream congregations. A few churches even borrowed from the restaurant trade and posted signs warning, "No shoes, no shirt, no service!" Thus, there was a scarcity of mature Christian leaders willing to take these brash, excited new believers under their wings and disciple them.

At the ripe old age of 26, I was considered by some of these kids as a "spiritual father."

With little seasoned leadership, the Jesus Movement suffered from youthful excesses and immaturity. As I look back today, it pains me that the church missed a tremendous opportunity simply because that opportunity came dressed in sloppy clothes.

So, as I considered God's promise of spiritual fatherhood in a future move of his Spirit, I was greatly encouraged.

Twenty-five years later God began to increasingly impress on me that the greater move he had spoken of was about to arrive. I felt him call me to be a voice in preparing his people for what he was about to do.

His words to me were direct and to the point: "Get my people ready for the harvest."

Over the next several weeks, as I prayed about my new assignment, the Lord gave me two objectives.

Objective One

One day I distinctly heard in my heart the Lord give me the command, "Build me an Ark."

I had no idea what he meant.

I went into one of the Sunday school classrooms at my church, found a picture of Noah's ark, brought it into my office, and taped it to the wall. It became a point of focus for me in my prayer times. But as I mulled over the familiar images of Noah hammering away on the hull, and animals going in two by two, I felt no closer to understanding the message.

Gradually I realized that the ark God wanted me to build was one of supportive relationships between churches, Christian businesses and organizations, and committed individuals -- uniting them into a great spiritual vessel that would hold and disciple the coming harvest.

As that realization took hold, I turned the word "ark" into an acronym that I believe reflects what God wants:

> An ALLIANCE of God's people
> who have been RENEWED by his Spirit
> to accomplish his KINGDOM purpose
> in the coming harvest. – **A.R.K.**

There must be a coming together of God's people, in all our various expressions of church and ministry, to finish the great commission. This is the primary goal of ARK.

Book Three of this series will deal more fully with the idea of the ARK and church unity. For now, it is enough to say that

God wants his church united in every city -- poised to enfold and disciple the lost who will flood in as he increasingly shakes the nations.

Objective Two

Not long after I heard God's first command, the second one came: "Build me the school of the prophets."

This was as puzzling to me as the command to build an ark. Nowhere in scripture does the literal expression "school of the prophets" appear. However, the Bible does speak of a prophetic training school, in the first book of Samuel. (1 Sam. 19:20)

Samuel led Israel through one of its greatest spiritual revivals. The Lord used him to gather hundreds of young prophets so that they might be trained to carry God's Word to Israel. I began to realize that God was calling me to do something similar.

Like Samuel, I was to raise up not only my voice but the voices of young prophetic leaders: calling God's people across the street – and around the world -- to readiness.

I believe God already is imparting to others his victorious paradigm, as he did with me. I have no exclusive franchise on this movement. And I am sure that the arks and the schools that emerge will take a variety of forms.

Their common denominator, however, will be committed young leaders, who respond to the swell of the harvest with a drive to prepare the church for discipling and shepherding.

How God wants us to create these arks and prophetic schools, I still do not fully know. There is no cookbook recipe or kit plan for performing these tasks.

But God has made one thing very clear to me: What he will do through them will far surpass *anything* we can imagine.

REVIEW OF CHAPTER ONE

1. The calling: God wants his church ready for the climactic end of this age of harvest, which will be fueled by the last "great shaking" of the nations.

2. As a whole, the church is unprepared for the coming harvest. Too many are blind to what God wants to do, and are thinking incorrectly about the end times. The hardest -- and yet, most fruitful -- days of the church are ahead.

3. The Lord is raising up many prophetic voices to begin awakening his church to what he is ready to do. These prophetic messengers must be encouraged, prepared, and sent. This is the purpose of the "School of the Prophets."

4. God wants A.R.K.'s built -- united churches and Christian organizations to create city-wide spiritual houses or containers for receiving and discipling the coming great harvest.

CHAPTER TWO

The Promised Shaking

People have asked me, "Why do you think the greatest harvest of the church is yet to come?" My answer is simple: because God is going to increasingly shake the nations until they see their need of his salvation in Jesus Christ.

It is important to understand that God's shaking is not focused on judgment, but on alerting the church and the people of the world that the end of time is almost at our doorstep.

God has one goal: to magnify his son and the redemption that Jesus has brought to the world. God wants the lost saved, and God is going to increasingly "turn up the heat" on the world to capture its attention.

Many have allowed themselves to see God as loving yet passive in his care for the world. The opposite is true.

As Jesus' parable of the lost sheep points out, it is the Lord himself who is going out to rescue and save those he loves. (Matt. 18:12; Lk.15:4)

I am in no way saying God will forego using the church in world evangelism. Jesus *is* going after the lost through his church. But we must not limit our view of God's sovereignty.

God will use every resource of his Kingdom to reach every man and woman with the good news.

Understanding The Coming Shaking

My expectations of the greatest harvest in church history aren't speculative. There is a solid biblical basis for such belief.

Study of Haggai 2

It is the prophet Haggai who coined the phase "the last shaking." But before we study Haggai's teaching, we should note that the prophet Joel was the first to refer to the idea -- 250 years earlier.

> Multitudes, multitudes in the valley of decision; for the day of the LORD is near in the valley of decision! The sun and the moon shall be darkened, and the stars shall gather in their light. The LORD shall also roar out of Zion and utter His voice from Jerusalem. **And the heavens and the earth shall shake.** But the LORD will be the hope of His people and the strength of the sons of Israel. (Joel 3:14-18 MKJV)

Even though Joel is the first to speak of the shaking, it is Haggai -- along with help from the writer of the Book of Hebrews -- who gives us our best understanding of God's redemptive purposes in it.

Haggai was one of two prophets sent by God to encourage the Jewish remnant that returned from the Babylonian captivity in the 5th Century B.C. to rebuild the Jerusalem temple. These returning Jews encountered internal discouragements and external threats as they sought to obey God in restoring the temple. Eventually it became more than they could endure.

For 16 years they stopped all work. It was during this period God raised up the prophets Zechariah and Haggai to preach to them, trying to motivate them to finish rebuilding the house of God.

One of the discouragements that stopped God's people from working on the post-exilic temple was comparing it to Solomon's temple. As they laid the new temple's foundations, old men – who had living memories of King Solomon's temple – broke down and wept: The new temple looked small and pitiful compared with the former temple. This caused many workers to lose heart.

But Haggai made an astonishing promise in Chapter 2 of his book: If the people would obey God and build this seemingly insignificant temple, God would bring the "desire of all nations" (the Messiah) to his restored house, and fill it with his manifest glory so that all the nations of the world would see, and be drawn to it (Hag. 2:6-7).

The prophet boldly declared "the glory of the latter house [the restored temple] would be greater than the former house [Solomon's temple]." (Hag. 2:9).

But God never filled that post-exilic temple with his glory so that the nations of the world were drawn to it. There is no way that Haggai's prophecy can be seen as having been fulfilled there.

Instead we find what we call a "double prophecy." [i] It was the will of God to build the post-exilic temple – but that building was only a shadow of a greater house of God in the distant future, which would bring God's salvation to the nations.

Hebrews 12:26-29

The writer of Hebrews provides us with insight into the double meaning in Haggai's prophecy. Haggai wrote that the Messiah's coming would bring greater glory to God's restored house than ever was seen in Solomon's temple. And this greater glory would arrive at the time of a second divine "shaking" of the nations.

In Hebrews 12:26 the writer translates Haggai's phrase "yet once" with the better translation of "yet once more."

> For so says Jehovah of hosts: Yet once, it is a little while, and I will shake the heavens, and the earth, and the sea, and the dry land. (Hag. 2:6 MKJV)
>
> ...whose voice then shook the earth: but now he hath promised, saying, Yet once more will I make to tremble not the earth only, but also the heavens... (Heb.12:26 MKJV)

"Yet once more" denotes a first shaking. In the creation of Israel, God had shaken Egypt -- the greatest nation of its era -- to its very foundations. Other nations were also affected as God led Israel to the promised land.

At Mount Sinai there was a literal shaking, at the base of the burning, cloud-covered mountain (Ex. 19:9-18). A nation was born and Israel became God's covenant people. But Haggai and the writer of Hebrews promised a greater shaking was coming that would dwarf the first.

This second shaking would be worldwide.

From it would proceed a greater covenant, with greater glory in the house of God than was ever seen in the temple of Solomon. In this greater house the peace of God would be found for all peoples. (Hag. 2:9)

The writer of Hebrews makes it clear that Haggai's prophetic promise of a greater divine visitation and glory was not fulfilled in the post-exilic temple or the later Herodian Temple. It was to be fulfilled in the formation of a different kind of temple -- the church -- which would manifest the "unshakable" Kingdom of God that came through Jesus Christ.

> The expression "once more" signifies the removal of what can be shaken, that is, what he has made, so that what cannot be shaken may remain. Therefore, since we are receiving a kingdom that cannot be shaken, let us be thankful and worship God in reverence and fear in a way that pleases him. (Heb.12:27-28)

This future shaking will cause events to happen in the heavens and on the earth that will undermine people's confidence in temporal, physical life. Social positions, money, land, political power – these will be meaningless as the fabric of the nations begins to unravel.

These God-caused shakings will start whole nations searching for what is unshakable. Through that search, many will discover that only through faith in Jesus Christ can we find an unshakable life here and now.

REVIEW OF CHAPTER TWO

1. God has produced two spiritual shakings in history. The first created the nation of Israel, which was to be his witness to the surrounding nations. The second shaking is ongoing: it has produced a worldwide witnessing church - declaring a universal covenant of salvation to all who will receive it. The shaking is still growing.

2. The Lord used the post-exilic temple to be a shadow of a greater end-times temple (the church), which would reveal his greater glory so nations would be drawn to the church's witness.

3. The last shaking will cause the nations to search for what is unshakable in life. As social, political, and physical sources of security begin to fail, people will seek for whatever will give them stability and hope. This is the launching of the great harvest.

CHAPTER THREE

The Shaking of the Earth

I was working in my church office when abruptly everything began to shake. I looked out the window and saw telephone wires bouncing up and down, the poles waving back and forth.

As the shaking persisted, I got up and stood in the doorway to my office, thinking it might be a safer place. Most of our church staff came to their office doorways, too, wearing worried expressions. Finally the shaking stopped.

We had just experienced the 1989 Loma Prieta earthquake, which was the biggest temblor to hit the San Francisco Bay Area in decades.

There were some aftershocks, but eventually those faded away. However, what stayed with me was the sense of *helplessness* I had felt. Everything firm, fixed, and predictable had suddenly gone into motion. There was no solid ground on which to stand, no steady wall on which to lean.

Scripture is clear that as we approach the end times God is going to increasingly bring physical, spiritual, and emotional shaking to the world. Our job is to be ready to reach out to those left fearful, bewildered, and helpless.

Haggai divides his prophecy of the last shaking into two parts. There will be a shaking of the earth, and a shaking of the heavens. I want to discuss these separately because each will make its own vital contribution to the climactic ending of the great harvest.

But first we must see that Jesus himself is one of the most impactful teachers on the end times shaking.

The Mount Olive Discourse

The "Mount Olive Discourse" in Matthew 24, Luke 21, and Mark 13 comes out of Jesus' reaction to his disciples admiring the beauty of the Herodian Temple as they walked through it. Jesus startles them by saying, "You see these stones, the day is coming when not one will be left on the other which will not be thrown down." (Lk. 21: 6)

The disciples reacted to Jesus' prediction by asking when his prophecy would be fulfilled, and what signs would precede this devastation.

At that moment, Jesus looked into the future and predicted some startling events. Some of these predictions focused on events close at hand, but some envisioned events that would happen only at his second coming. What is important is that Jesus ties his predictions to the promised shaking.

> And there shall be signs in the sun, and in the moon, and in the stars. And on the earth will be anxiety of nations with perplexity; the sea and the waves roaring; men fainting from fear, and expecting those things which have come on the earth. For the powers of the heavens shall be shaken. (Luke 21:25-26)

Let's examine in order what Jesus sees as happening in this great and last shaking of the nations:

1) The shaking will accelerate through the Age of the Church.

It is clear in Jesus' prediction that the shaking would stretch from the time of the early church to his second coming. Jesus' prophecy of the destruction of the Herodian Temple came to pass in 70 A.D., early in the life of the church. But obviously, most of his predictions will come to pass at the time of his second coming. (Matt. 24:30; Mk.13:26; Lk. 21:27) As the Kingdom of God grows and reaches its greatest expression, so will the shaking of the earth and the heavens increase.

2) A time of increasing deception.

Jesus' second prediction speaks of increasing religious deception. He warns his church to be alert to the appearances of false Christs seeking to deceive. (Mk. 13:5-6; Matt. 24:4-5,11; Lk. 21:8) Jesus gives the command to "take heed" -- warning us to be on guard against such deception.

3) A time of increasing wars, famines, plagues, and earthquakes.

Jesus' next prediction was of increasing worldwide wars, plagues and hunger, and natural disasters. The witness of the church will be presented in an age of growing violence and suffering. In the midst of such turmoil, the church will be challenged to bring God's peace, healing, and hope in the name of Christ. (Matt. 24:6-7; Mk. 13:7-8; Lk. 21:9-11) Mark and Matthew declare that these terrible events are the "beginning of labor pains" pointing to the approaching end of this age. (Mk. 13:7-8)

4) The suffering of the church in its redemptive work.

Jesus warns his church to "be alert" to the negative reactions of many to the gospel, and to the cost the church will pay in proclaiming this message. He makes it clear that part of the church's witness of God's sacrificial love for the world is its willingness to suffer for the sake of the gospel. (Mk. 13:9: Matt. 24:9)

Paul teaches the churches in his care to not be shaken when such times of persecution arise:

> Therefore, when we could stand it no longer, we decided to remain alone in Athens and send Timothy, our brother who works with us for God in the gospel of Christ, to strengthen and encourage you in your faith, so that no one would be shaken by these persecutions, for which you are aware that we were destined. In fact, when we were with you, we told you ahead of time that we were going to suffer persecution. And as you know, that is what happened. (1 Thess.3:1-4 ISV)

More and more the church will need to review what Jesus said when he told us that as his disciples we will need to "count the cost." (Lk. 14:27-28) We must be careful not to teach people that Jesus always makes life better, more enjoyable, and safer. To stand for Christ can cost us dearly.

Yet, in the midst of the church's suffering, God will grant "inner peace" (Phil. 4:7) and "patient endurance." (Lk. 21:19) The Holy Spirit will inspire his people to give powerful testimonies as they stand before rulers. Such rulers will be unable to refute the wisdom that God imparts in those challenging moments. (Lk. 21:12-16) The church is not going to run from the coming fight. Persecution will release a new level of purity and power into its witness.

5) The righteous will not suffer the judgments of the wicked.

In the midst of prophesying the sufferings of the church, Jesus points out that it will not suffer the judgments of the wicked. Jesus declares that "not one hair" will be lost on the head of God's people due to divine judgment. (Lk. 21:18)

For example, Jesus clearly predicts that Jerusalem will be destroyed because of the Jews' rejection of their Messiah. (Lk. 19:43-44; 21:21-25) Yet in the destruction of Jerusalem there is no record of the death of Christians.

There is a tradition that as the Roman armies marched up to Jerusalem, the whole Jerusalem church escaped the city. [ii] Jesus exhorts us to pray so that we will be alert to such coming judgments on the wicked. As they arrive, we are to consider how to avoid them. (Mk. 13:8)

Notice that during God's judgment on the nation of Egypt in sending the ten plagues, none of them touched the Hebrews. (Ex. 8:22; 9:26) Paul is clear in his first letter to the Thessalonians that "God did not choose us to suffer his anger..." (1 Thess. 5:9 GNB) As we stay alert in the last days, we will have nothing to fear from the Lord.

6) Persecution and worldly distractions will cause spiritual backsliding.

There will be spiritual decline and the need for renewal among God's people. Jesus warned that as wickedness (lawlessness) increased, the love of many would grow cold (Matt. 24:10,12; Lk. 8:13-14).

This "cold love" is what the Apostle John contrasts to our "first love," in which we begin our walk with Christ with a passionate heart to love and serve him.

In this passage, Jesus refers to believers who will no longer have a desire to please or obey the Lord; instead they will desire to serve themselves, and even justify living in sin. The Apostle Paul speaks of this great falling away in his second letter to the Thessalonians:

> Let not anyone deceive you by any means. For that Day shall not come unless there first comes a falling away, and the man of sin shall be revealed, the son of perdition..." (2 Th. 2:3)

Paul is telling the Thessalonians that this falling away will be so pronounced that the church will recognize it as a sign of Christ's imminent return. In Paul's letter to his spiritual son Timothy, he again brings up this great falling away.

> But the Spirit expressly says that in the latter times some shall depart from the faith, giving heed to seducing spirits and teachings of demons... (1 Tim. 4:1)

Book Two of this series will deal more with the need for renewal in the last-days church, and outline how God will launch a counter-move of revival that will see many backslidden believers restored.

Our take-away here, however, is that Jesus anticipates the struggle of the end-times church to stay faithful amidst growing persecution and spiritual lawlessness. This must become one of our highest priorities.

7) The unstoppable gospel.

Jesus' last prediction in the Mount Olive Discourse speaks of the church reaching every nation with the gospel message. (Matt. 24:14) As the shaking of the nations increases, there will be an unprecedented harvest of souls, with the gospel powerfully advancing throughout the world.

This last prediction is almost complete. We will confirm in Book Three of this series that the church is experiencing hundreds of thousands being brought into the Kingdom of God daily. Jesus' predictions are coming to pass.

The Sign Of The Fig Tree

In all three gospel accounts of Jesus' Mount Olive Discourse, he highlights the parable of the fig tree. Jesus says, "When you see the fig tree put forth its leaves, you know that summer is near." (Matt. 24:32-35; Mk. 13:28; Lk. 21:29-31)

Jesus is clear that the fig tree will be a strong sign of the near fulfillment of his predictions.

Scripture is consistent in identifying Israel as a fig tree. (Hos. 9:10; Jer. 24:1-10; Lk. 13:6-9) Many bible teachers see this parable referring to the restoration of Israel as a nation at the end of this age, and a sign of his imminent return.

Israel ceased to be a nation after the destruction of Jerusalem in 70 A.D. But Jesus predicted that the restoration of Israel as a sovereign country would happen before his return. (Lk. 21:24)

Jesus' prediction has come to pass. Israel became a nation again in 1948 and gained control of Jerusalem after the Six Day War in 1967. The "fig tree" was replanted, and it has been "putting forth its leaves" for over 67 years.

The Witness Of The Seven Seals

Sixty years after the death of Jesus, the Apostle John received a revelation that reinforced Jesus' Mount Olive predictions.

In the Book of Daniel, Daniel was instructed to "seal up" the revelation that God had given him of the judgments on mankind that would happen at the end of time. (Dan. 12:4) But with Jesus' coming, we see this closed book reopened.

As an old man in exile on the island of Patmos, John was given a great vision of the resurrected Jesus again unfolding God's long-hidden plan of salvation and judgment for humanity. The breadth of this vision is captured in the Book of Revelation in Chapters 5 and 6.

I won't try to exegete these chapters in detail, but I want to compare them to Jesus' Mount Olive Discourse to show how consistent they are with what Jesus predicted.

The Opening Of The Seals

The opening of the seals has to do with the willingness of Jesus to offer himself as our "sin sacrifice," purchasing the right for us to know God and his redemptive plan (Rev. 5:1-7). John in his vision sees Jesus pictured as the worthy slain lamb with "seven horns and seven eyes," meaning the resurrected Christ now has perfect strength and revelation for his Church.

It is important for us to understand that it is the slain lamb who opens the seals. Jesus does not use his position as the conquering king to reveal salvation history. The story of the seals is not about the reigning Christ, but about the worthy redeemer who is seeking to save and restore a broken, sin-sick world.

With the opening of the seals comes the story of redemption and judgment that will spread across the earth through the finished work of Christ. Though John speaks of seven seals, I only want to deal with the first six — which closely parallel Jesus' Mount Olive predictions. The seventh seal is distinct from the others, and its breaking unleashes a new, separate series of judgments.

1) The First Seal. In this we see the spread of false Christian teaching, attempting to distort the gospel and deceive the nations. Some have characterized this first seal as showing Jesus going forth to conquer through the spread of the gospel, and being victorious. I know of several Bible commentators who like this interpretation; but I do not agree with them. Nowhere else in scripture is Jesus pictured with a bow. Satan is spoken of as using "fiery darts or arrows" of temptation. (Eph. 6:16) Almost always Jesus' weapon of choice is the "sword of his mouth." (Eph. 6:17; Heb. 4:12; Rev. 1:16; 2:16; 19:15, 21) Notice that one of the first things Jesus warns his disciples about in his Olivet discourse is "deception." This deception would come in the form of those trying to impersonate Jesus. (Matt. 24:4-5; Mark 13:5-6; Lk. 21:8) Consequently, I believe the first seal is the recognition of the rise of false and deceiving

messiahs trying to form false doctrine to distort the image and message of Christ. (6:2)

2) The Second Seal is what Jesus predicted of wars and rumors of wars that will increase over the age of the church. (6:3-4)

3) The Third Seal deals with the growing devastation of famines on the earth. (6:5-6)

4) The Fourth Seal deals with disease (plagues) resulting from natural devastations (earthquakes) that will lead to more war and famine destroying large populations of people on the earth. (6:7-8) The phrase "death and hell" literally means "death and destruction" following these events.

5) The Fifth Seal deals with the incredible persecution that will increasingly happen to the church, resulting in many martyrs for the faith. (6:9-11) Jesus addresses this issue at length, and describes what this persecution will look like.

6) The Sixth Seal deals with climactic earthly and heavenly shaking events that leads to Jesus' second coming. (6:12-17; Mk. 13:24-27)

The only variance from Jesus' Mount Olive discourse is in John's seeming omission of the gospel's victorious advance into all nations. However, a careful look reveals that John does point to the worldwide end time witness of the church.

The word "testimony" in Revelation 6:9 is "marturia," from which we get the word "martyr," meaning "witness." The idea of the witnessing world church is referenced here, but it has a negative focus -- dealing with how much longer

Antichrist will be allowed to continue the persecution of the church.

Jesus responds to the question from the heavenly martyrs by saying that the church's witness must continue a little longer, with even more "martyrs" destined to lay down their lives for the gospel. The obvious unspoken thought is that there are still unbelievers who will have a chance to be saved.

We can see that John's predictions closely follow Jesus' predictions. These two lists help us understand what the coming shaking on earth will look like.

The Need For An Unshakable Kingdom

The growing shaking of the nations has one goal: to awaken the nations to their need of God's salvation. I encourage you to look at Appendix Three for a modern example of God's shaking of the Middle East -- releasing a wave of salvation in a previously unreachable people group.

From this review of what God's end-time shaking will look like, we can see why the writer of Hebrews speaks about the need of receiving an "unshakable" life in Christ. (Heb. 12: 27-28) Many will seek whatever can bring stability and hope.

Jesus speaks of the growing despair of the world as the shaking comes to its climax. He states that there will be "anxiety of nations," "worldwide perplexity," and "men's hearts fainting with fear." (Lk. 21: 25-26) Eventually all nations will realize that God is behind these shaking judgments. (Rev. 16:9)
The wicked will respond with hatred toward God and his church. (Matt. 24:9; Rev. 16:9, 11) Yet this period of time will

be one the greatest opportunities for the mission of the church. (Lk. 21: 13) Mighty works of the Holy Spirit will be evident, (Lk. 21:14-15), and the greatest worldwide outpouring of the Spirit will strengthen and empower the church.

From this worldwide upheaval will come the astonishing harvest wave that will climax the end of this age. The Lord wants his church ready to deal with it.

REVIEW OF CHAPTER THREE

1. This chapter pictures what the shaking of the earth will look like, as characterized in the prophecies of both Jesus and the Apostle John.

2. In the Mount Olive Discourse, Jesus offers a clear picture of the increased physical shaking of the earth over the age of the church. It shows the impact of deception and persecution, as well as world evangelism, as we draw closer to the second coming of Christ. Jesus is warning the church how to prepare.

3. The Sign of the Fig Tree is a key indicator of when Jesus' predictions will come to fruition. The Fig Tree represents Israel becoming a nation again, with its rule over Jerusalem being restored in the last days.

4. Jesus' and John's predictions show why the world will be perplexed and searching for answers. We can see how God will use this last shaking to stir up the great harvest.

Chapter Four

The Shaking of the Heavens

In 1988 I was standing on a baseball field in the middle of our city, surrounded by about 40 other ministers. We had been assembled by several well-known pastors from South America.

These pastors had taught us that we needed to "bind" the strong demonic powers over our city, so that we might release our churches to dramatically reach the lost.

For around 45 minutes we prayed, shouted, and sought to identify these powers by name and bind them.

As I reflect back on our earnest effort, led by these gracious South American pastors, I now realize we were accomplishing -- nothing.

Jesus Christ has already defeated Satan. The church is not responsible for defeating him "more." We must simply believe what Jesus did for us on the cross, and act like it.

When an air force destroys an enemy's air power, then it remains for the infantry to go in and take the land. The infantry doesn't have to fight its own battle with the opposing air force. That threat is already neutralized.

Jesus Christ is our air power, and his victory was complete and total. Today, the army of God is free to take the ground Satan possessed -- knowing we have a secure heaven above us.

The Taking Of The Heavens

Both Haggai and the writer of Hebrews stressed that the coming shaking will rock not only the earth, but also the heavens. Many believe this reference to "shaking the heavens" refers to the cosmic events that will happen as we approach the great and terrible day of the Lord.

> And immediately after the tribulation of those days, the sun shall be darkened and the moon shall not give her light, and the stars shall fall from the heaven, and the powers of the heavens shall be shaken." (Matt. 24:29)

> I will show wonders in the heavens above and signs on the earth below blood and fire and billows of smoke. The sun will be turned to darkness and the moon to blood before the coming of the great and glorious day of the Lord. (Acts 2:19-20)

The Bible makes it clear that this age will end with the convulsing of the cosmos, which will indeed be part of the last shaking. But there is a spiritual dimension of God's heavenly shaking as well as a physical dimension.

Remember, the overall purpose of the great shaking is redemptive, not just judgment and destruction. It is God releasing or allowing events that will cause the unsaved to begin looking for him.

Over this age of harvest, God's shaking will more and more awaken the nations to see his visible glory in his end-times temple, the church. (Hag. 2:7) Therefore, the shaking of the heavens will also aid in producing the harvest.

The Fall Of Satan

It is important to understand that God's second shaking, which began with the coming of Jesus Christ, shook Satan out of the second heaven. This shaking of Satan caused the beginning of a reversal of spiritual control over the earth.

Satan now resides in the first heaven, or what we call the atmosphere surrounding the earth. I realize God's spiritual rule of the first heaven will not be complete until Jesus comes again, but because of Christ, the church has now become the dominant spiritual force in the heavenlies.

Three Heavens

The Bible indicates there are three heavens, or places where spiritual beings reside. The Apostle Paul in his second letter to the Corinthian Church refers to someone being spiritually taken up into the "third" heaven, where God dwells. (2 Cor. 12:2) This seems to be the highest heaven, because it is God's home.

In Ezekiel 28:14 we discover through a prophetic poem that Satan at one time had been a covering angel (a cherub) who lived in the third heaven near the throne of God. But at some point he was cast out because of a rebellion he led against God. (Ezk. 28:16; Rev. 12:4) Satan then dropped to a "second" heaven, where he seems to still have some limited access to God, and retains some degree of heavenly power or influence.

Because of the sin of Adam, Satan became the "ruler" of this world. (Jn. 12:31-32; 14:30). In the temptation of Jesus, Satan boasts, "I will give you all their authority and splendor (the worldly kingdoms); it has been given to me, and I can give it to anyone I want to..." (Lk. 4:6).

Please note: Jesus does *not* dispute Satan's claim.

As a ruler, Satan was able to impose his will on the earth, to a limited degree. We see him coming before God to accuse God's servants. (Job. 1:6-11; Rev. 12:10) He terrorized humanity with his power of death and hell (destruction). (Heb. 2:14-15; Rev. 1:18) And he could interfere with the arrival of answered prayer. (Dan. 10:13)

These few passages do not give us a complete picture of Satan's authority in the second heavens, but we can discern that it was a significant position of power set against the purposes of God. (For a better understanding of the fall of Satan from the different heavens, refer to Appendix Two.)

With the resurrection and exaltation of Jesus Christ, however, we see a shaking of the spiritual realm!

Satan now is pictured as being thrown out of his position of power over humanity. (Rev. 12:7-10; Lk. 10:18-19; Col. 2:15) There is no longer an accuser of God's people before God in the heavens. (Rom. 8:1) Jesus has become the stronger spiritual power, able to rob Satan's house and destroy the works of his kingdom. (Lk. 11:21-22, 1 Jn. 3:8)

Now, Jesus as the head of his church, and its high priest, has taken the highest seat in heaven to intercede for believers. (Eph. 1:20-22; Heb.8:1)

One of the most spectacular works of God in Christ was his positioning of believers in the highest heaven in Christ at God's right hand. (Eph. 2:6; Col. 3:1) He has given us incredible access to God in prayer and authority to declare things on earth as they are in heaven. (Matt. 6:10) I want you to look at the amazing prayer triangle that every believer has been given through Jesus Christ.

Jesus our High Priest intercedes and advocates for us. Heb. 7:24-25

God responds to Jesus' intercession. 1 Jn. 5:14-15

The Holy Spirit intercedes and helps us to pray. Rom. 8:26-27

This amazing prayer relationship is the product of the New Covenant in Jesus Christ.

Our connection to God is radically different from that of the Old Testament saints. We can now spiritually stand before God, at his throne. (Heb. 4:16) Satan can no longer interpose himself between us and God to interfere with our prayers.

With the leading of the Holy Spirit we can become partners with God in his shaking of the nations.

Partners In The Heavenly Shaking

The battle for the heavens has been won. Jesus has been given the highest place in the highest heaven. And we have been included in that exaltation. God has given us tremendous authority to manifest his kingdom on earth, as it is in heaven, through our prayer and our testimony.

> Truly, truly, I say to you, He who believes on Me, the works that I do he shall do also, and greater works than these he shall do, because I go to My Father. And whatever you may ask in My name, that I will do, so that the Father may be glorified in the Son. If you ask anything in My name, I will do it. (Jn. 14:12-14 MKJV)

> Truly I say to you, whatever you shall bind on earth shall occur, having been bound in Heaven; and whatever you shall loose on earth shall occur, having been loosed in Heaven. Again I say to you that if two of you shall agree on earth as regarding anything that they shall ask, it shall be done for them by My Father in Heaven." (Matt. 18:18-19 MKJV)

Jesus has given the church permission to pray as our circumstances may require. As we bring the kingdom of God into cities and neighborhoods, we can in a real sense "legislate" in prayer what is needed to reveal the kingdom and fully declare the gospel.

I understand that it may seem in these two previous verses that Jesus is giving license to the church to use its position in

Christ to get anything it may want in prayer, but this is not true. The qualifying verse is found in the Apostle John's first letter:

> And this is the confidence that we have toward Him, that if we ask anything <u>according to His will</u>, He hears us. And if we know that He hears us, whatever we ask, we know that we have the petitions that we desired of Him." (1Jn. 5:14-15)

The key phrase here is "according to his will." We cannot just ask whatever we want; our prayers need to reflect God's will, not our own. Jesus states "your will be done on earth as it is in heaven." (Matt. 6:10) But as long as we are careful to discover the will of God in any situation on earth, we can bring the kingdom of God into it with great power.

Binding And Loosing

In the verse I just quoted in Matthew 18:18 there is the mention of God giving the church "binding and loosing power." I want to clarify the authority that God has given to us to help in the great heavenly shaking and the shaping of the coming harvest.

The phrase "binding and loosing" actually has the meaning of "prohibit" and "allow." Again, some believers have misunderstood it to think that Jesus is giving the church the power to determine what on earth will be allowed or prohibited. This is incorrect. Let me explain by reviewing some of Jesus' teaching:

> I will give you the keys of the Kingdom of

53

heaven; what you prohibit on earth will be prohibited in heaven, and what you permit on earth will be permitted in heaven." (Matt. 16:19 GNB)

And if he will not listen to them, then tell the whole thing to the church. Finally, if he will not listen to the church, treat him as though he were a pagan or a tax collector. And so I tell all of you: what you prohibit on earth will be prohibited in heaven, and what you permit on earth will be permitted in heaven." (Matt. 18:17-18 GNB)

Properly understood, these two passages reveal the church's authority to "declare" things on earth that are consistent with God's will in heaven. In the Hebrew-Greek Key Study Bible in the footnote for Matthew 16:18 is written –

The two verbs, *dedemenon* (bind) and *lelymenon* (loose), are both perfect passive participles, which can be translated respectively as "having been bound" and "having been loosed" already. Those things which have been conclusively determined by God are revealed by the church on earth. Believers therefore only announce that which confirms those decisions which already have been made by God.[iii]

It is important that we recognize not only the authority that God has given us in Christ, but also our limitations. We have great power to establish *God's* will on earth – not our own. In Matthew 16 we see Jesus giving the church "the keys of the

Kingdom," which are to be used to open the Gates of Hades. The concept of Hades here is the satanic power to blind the eyes of the lost to the gospel. (2 Cor.4:3-4; Jn. 12:39) But no longer can Satan and his kingdom lock the church out from reaching the lost. When the church goes into a city or region, it has the authority to confront and demolish demonic lies that have blinded people for generations. (2 Cor. 10:4)

The church also has the power to open heavenly doors by using God-given authority to preach and show forth the power of the kingdom of God.

We can bind demonic forces and open the ears of the spiritually deaf, because this is in agreement with what has already been done in heaven.

Targeting The Shaking

Understanding the position and authority of the church in prayer allows us, as God's workers, to assist in the last shaking. More specifically, we can *target* the shaking.

God knows that to take and secure an area you must have "boots on the ground." This is the idea behind the great commission – Jesus won the "air war," but we must take the victory to the streets of cities and neighborhoods around the world.

Let me take my military illustration further. Since we "own the air" we can now "call in air strikes." Let's say God calls you to minister within an inner-city neighborhood. You move into the neighborhood and begin to spiritually survey what is going on. You identify where Satan has established strongholds of sin, such as drug addiction, gang activity, or sex trade.

You know that God's will is to destroy such works of the devil. (1 Jn. 3:8) So you gather God's people to pray, and you target key drug lords, gangs, or pimps. With determined and persistent prayer you take authority over these evil leaders and their groups, "binding up" their work, and forbidding it to continue. You can also "loose" law enforcement to come and break up these evil organizations.

What you are doing is focusing God's desired shaking of that inner city. You are God's agent to identify where some of his spiritual shaking will occur.

Taking Action

But along with targeted prayer must come targeted action to capitalize on the prayer effort.

Staying with our example, along with targeted prayer we would take the opportunity to launch outreaches to gang members in jail, and reach out to their families. It also would be effective to launch after-school bible clubs to touch kids of addicted parents, or of gang members.

Because the air war is won, we are free to move into Satan-held regions with the power to manifest the kingdom of God.

Will Satan push back? Yes. But he has no real power against God's people. He cannot use the power of binding and loosing against us. He uses fear, the hate and pain in the hearts of people, and deception.

He can stir up persecution and create frustrating

circumstances; but a determined, united, praying, and Spirit-empowered church will overcome these tactics. When we know who we are and what we have in Christ, we refuse to let the enemy behave as if his defeat by Jesus wasn't already accomplished. We must know better.

The Growing World Prayer Movement

As we come to understand the incredible authority the Lord has given the church through prayer, it is important to awaken the church to how God wants to use it in shaking the nations.

As I researched what has been happening with prayer around the world, I discovered that one of the most powerful prayer movements in church history is forming. A number of "prayer initiatives" have been launched over the last two decades, which are bringing together *millions* of believers globally to focus on key people groups.[iv]

Many of these prayer-mission movements share two common denominators: they want to raise up thousands of "houses of prayer" that are praying 24/7; and they want to provide ministries of healing and deliverance on the ground for the people groups they target.[v]

With modern communications, there is no limit to how many of God's people can pray in unity. One initiative, called "Light the Window," aims to link 10 million intercessors to pray for the peoples of the 10/40 window through the year 2020. The goal is to generate up to one *billion* hours of prayer for spiritual breakthrough among 365 of the largest unreached people groups, comprising about 2.5 billion people. [1]

These numbers are startling in that so many can be focused in prayer. But let me offer a cautioning word: Researchers like George Otis, Jr., known for his exciting *Transformation* video series, are documenting that *who* is praying, and *how* they are praying, are truly key to seeing a great move of God. Just a few fervent, committed, believing intercessors can jump-start astonishing transformations.

I would agree with Jonathan, the son of the first king of Israel, who declared, "for there is no restraint to Jehovah to save by many or by few." (1 Sam.14:6) Whether God uses millions or a few dedicated prayer warriors, Jesus has won the air war for his church and we need to exercise our God-given authority.

How Satan Can Still Resist The Church

Though scripture shows that Jesus has won the position of power in the heavens, it doesn't mean that Satan is helpless to resist the church and frustrate its commission. The battle remains real and deadly. Satan has simply changed his tactics.

The Apostle Paul writes that we must not be ignorant of the devil's devices and strategies. (2 Cor. 2:11; Eph. 6:11) Satan can resist the work of the church through persecution, lies, deception, sinning saints, and church division. Let me review three primary attacks of the devil on God's people.

1. Ignorance of the Word of God

Biblical ignorance is a powerful tool in Satan's hands. The

---

1 David Taylor. "Intercessory Missions." *Mission Frontiers*. (July/August, 2014); Vol.36. No.4, p.5

prophet Hosea wrote that God's people get in trouble when they "lack knowledge" of his word (Hos. 4:6). Satan can lie to us very convincingly and use the misunderstandings we have about ourselves and about God to defeat us. (2 Cor. 11:14-15)

There is a saying: "God can use an ignorant man; he just can't use his ignorance." We must know from God's word what we have in Christ, and who he has made us to be.

Much of the confusion, division, and defeat we see in the church today is not the result of Satan's authority blocking the church, but of saints believing demonic lies that take them out of the battle. When we fail to realize that God has made us new creatures and that we are no longer who we used to be, we are left defeated and confused.

2. Sinning Saints

Paul warns believers "not to give the devil an opportunity" by continuing to sin. (Eph. 4:27)

Sinning saints will destroy their prayer effectiveness, in that God will not respond to their prayers. (Ps. 66:18; 1 Pet. 3:7) We must keep our hearts right with God, and build a confessional life that constantly deals with temptations to sin.

Every believer needs an "accountability partner" with whom they regularly share their hearts and their struggles. Such disciplines keep the enemy from gaining footholds. (Eph. 4:27)

3. Church Division

Jesus is clear: A house divided against itself cannot stand. (Matt. 12:25; Mk. 3:25) God has told us to "make every effort" to keep the unity of the Holy Spirit in the bond of peace. (Eph. 4:3) We have no excuse *not* to be united with other churches and Christian organizations in our efforts to evangelize cities and neighborhoods for Christ.

Satan uses the sin of division to frustrate the great commission. When we ask God to send workers into the harvest field (Matthew 9: 37-38), God is free to send whom he sees as best to send – not whom we might prefer.

Too many times we reject whom God sends to help us, because they wear the wrong label, or we fear we might lose sheep to them. Seek first his kingdom (please the Lord in what you're doing) and all these things (what you truly need) will be given to you! (Matt. 6:33)

The Unstoppable Church

When God's people are determined to humble their hearts toward one another and unite around essential doctrine (Eph. 4:4-6), together focusing on the great commission under the leading of the Holy Spirit, then Satan and his angels cannot long resist. There is nothing more powerful than a united church.

Concerted, persistent prayer and evangelism are changing the spiritual environment over entire cites, regions, and nations. The growing world prayer movement is lining up millions of believers to pray using 21st century technology.

It is time for the Church to take its heavenly place in shaking the earth and bringing forth the great harvest.

1. It is true that God will shake the stars and planets to alert the world to the imminence of Jesus' second coming. But the main focus of the last heavenly shaking was to destroy the demonic control of Satan over mankind. The heavenly shaking of God through the finished works of Christ at the cross destroyed Satan's position of power over humanity. This power position has been given to Jesus and his church.

2. Having been raised, in Christ, to a position of heavenly authority in prayer, God's people can participate in the strategic shaking of nations. They can pray the will of God down on earth as it is in heaven. The church now has the power to permit or prohibit things on earth according to the will of God.

3. The worldwide prayer movement, using modern communications, can link an incredible number of believers in prayer – impacting whole nations and people groups.

4. Satan can still resist the church by using our disunity and sinful living to frustrate the work of intercession and our witness to the world. The church is becoming an unstoppable force, but we must recognize the need of renewal, and unity, to maintain momentum in the great harvest.

PART TWO

The Great Harvest

We, the church, have received the great commission to go into all nations, bearing witness to the love and saving message of God through Jesus Christ. As we go, we are to expect a growing response to our witness.

This is what the Bible calls the "harvest." (Jn. 4:35) For over 2000 years, the church has been harvesting people into the Kingdom of God.

Scripture is clear that as we approach the end of time, the speed and scope of harvesting will increase exponentially. Part Two deals with how this harvesting has indeed become a global phenomenon.

CHAPTER FIVE

The Age of Harvest

Jesus saw the questioning looks from his disciples as they returned from buying food and found him talking with a Samaritan woman.

The Jews hated the Samaritans, regarding them as a spiritually polluted people. Normally they avoided all contact with them. But Jesus, who had been resting by the town well while he waited for the disciples, knew God had arranged this meeting.

The Father had given him great insight into this woman's life. He watched as the Holy Spirit drew her heart to faith in him as the Messiah. He was filled with joy. His hunger was gone. This was what he had come for -- to bring the lost to faith in God.

After the woman left, the disciples encouraged Jesus to eat; but Jesus surprised them again. He said he had eaten food they did not yet understand.

The food that satisfied his soul was to do the will of God, and that was to cause people to believe in him as the Savior promised in scripture. Jesus exhorted his disciples to open their eyes, look beyond their prejudices, and see a vast harvest field of people ready to enter the kingdom of God through faith in him.

What Is The "Harvest"?

The harvest of God is the gathering of every man, woman, boy and girl – and creation itself – into God's kingdom, through faith in the message and work of Jesus Christ.

God has always had it in his heart to bring fallen man, and creation, back into a redeemed relationship with himself. (Gen. 3:15, Gen. 12:3-4; Rom. 8:19-22)

In Genesis 3:15 we find that Adam and Eve's sin broke fellowship with God, causing humanity to lose its righteous connection to him and to fall under the control of Satan. Yet, after losing the right to fellowship with God, Adam and his wife received the divine promise that through "the seed of woman" God would crush the head of Satan, releasing humanity from Satan's control. (Gen. 3:15)

From Genesis to Revelation, scripture tracks the salvation story of how God raised up first an individual, then a family, then a tribe, then a nation, and finally an international body of believers -- called the church -- to bring all nations into a saving relationship with God through Christ. (Gen. 12:3-4; Jn. 3:16)

God loves us, and he wants to not only rescue us from our sin nature, but to fulfill his original purpose of making us sons and daughters in his divine family. (Heb. 2:10; Rom. 8:29) To accomplish this he has gone to great lengths to provide salvation through Jesus Christ. Jesus emphatically declared that the saving of humanity is God's heart and purpose in human history:

...I have food to eat which you do not know. Therefore the disciples said to one another, No one brought Him anything to eat? Jesus said to them, My food is to do the will of Him who sent Me and to finish His work. Do you not say, It is yet four months, and the harvest comes? Behold, I say to you, Lift up your eyes and look on the fields, for they are white to harvest already. (Jn. 4:32-35)

In Matt. 9:38, Jesus describes God the Father as the "Lord of the harvest." The harvest is the focus of God. This must be our focus, too.

Jesus states that God's harvest work is divided into two parts: "harvest sowing" and "harvest reaping." (Jn. 4:36-38) God sends his people to speak into the lives of individuals (sowing), with the hope of people believing this message, acting on it and finding eternal life (reaping).

Everything Jesus did -- the calling and preparing of his disciples, his teachings, his signs and wonders and the sending of the Holy Spirit upon his church -- was for the express purpose of the salvation of lost humanity (Mk. 16:15-20; Acts 1:8).

The Symbolism Of Pentecost

The spiritual empowerment of the church on the day of Pentecost, the Feast of First Fruits, was no accident.

Pentecost means "50 days," which refers to the bringing in of the "first fruits" of the harvest 50 days after the Feast of Passover (Deut. 16:9-11). In late fall there was another festival, called the Feast of Tabernacles, to commemorate Israel's 40 years in the wilderness and to celebrate the bringing in of the final harvest (Lev. 23:40-43).

The implication is clear: The early church was the first fruit of this harvest age, 50 days after Jesus (our Passover lamb) was offered. (1 Cor. 5:7) Now we are waiting to celebrate the "final" harvest at the spiritual Feast of Tabernacles at the end of this age.

The last two millennia have been the "Age of Harvest." This is the time of fulfilling Jesus' Great Commission of going to all nations and preaching the gospel of the kingdom. (Matt. 28:18-20; Mk. 16:15) We await the finale, which is pictured in Revelation 14:16, where Jesus (through his corporate Body) will bring in the final harvest.

The Harvest Is Ready And Ripe

We need to see that with the coming of Jesus, God was announcing that the world harvest was ready to be brought in (Jn. 4:35-36). There was no need to wait for humanity to ripen further in its readiness to respond to the gospel. To illustrate this, Jesus made an observation about John the Baptist's mission:

> From the days of John the Baptist until the present, the kingdom of heaven has been forcefully advancing, and violent people have been attacking it, because the Law and all the Prophets prophesied up to the time of John. If you are willing to accept it, he is Elijah who is to come. Let the person who has ears listen. (Matt. 11:12-15 ISV)

Jesus was saying that from the beginning of John the Baptist's preaching, the kingdom was at last open. Crowds went out to John, rushing to hear the word of God through him and to respond to his message. (Matt. 3:5)

The spiritually hungry were ready to surge forward with remarkable intensity. After a 400-year wait, the prophetic silence had been broken. The harvest door was open, the harvest was pressing in – and it would continue doing so until the end of this age.

Resistant Harvest Fields

It would not be right to speak of a ripe harvest field and ignore the fact that some cities and people groups will not respond to the gospel.

Anyone who has tried to grow a church, or who has done evangelism, has come across what some call a "spiritually resistant" place where people seem inoculated against the gospel. Jesus predicted this. In fact, in his own ministry there were occasions when his message was resisted even by the people he grew up with (Lk. 4:16-31), and by cities where he did some of his greatest miracles. (Lk. 10:10-16)

In the context of Luke 10:1-12 and Matt. 10:1-15, Jesus instructs his disciples about going into the harvest field (Matt. 9:36-38; Lk. 10:2). He tells them how they are to handle rejection by any who spurn their message.

We will cover this more in Book Three of our series, but it is important to clarify that Jesus is not speaking of people who are simply struggling to understand the gospel. No, the people Jesus is instructing his disciples to walk away from are those who choose not to believe the gospel message even after the confirmation of signs and wonders.

It is crucial that we do harvesting the way Jesus carefully taught his disciples to do it. Jesus outlined five actions for them to take in dealing with a determined rejection of the gospel.

Five Actions In The Face Of Determined Unbelief

First, we need to be sure we are in the harvest field God has assigned to us. God prepares his servants for a specific harvest field. We do not choose our harvest field, God does.

Second, we must continue to pray the harvest prayer: "Pray that the Lord of the harvest send out his laborers into the harvest." There are key people in the place you are being sent who can make the difference in reaching it. (Lk. 10:2, 11) They may be believers, or not -- but they are chosen of God to help you. Certainly, they must decide whether to receive you. But if they do, the gospel has a foothold.

Third, it is crucial to bring the demonstration of the kingdom of God close to those in our harvest field. (Lk. 10:7-8) Jesus instructs the disciples to heal the sick, cast out demons, preach the gospel in the power of the Holy Spirit - to demonstrate of the reality of the kingdom. (Lk. 10:9,11) Such signs as the Holy Spirit grants to our witness will release a greater grace to those watching. People and cities who have seen the signs of the kingdom are held to a higher standard of responsibility than those who have not. (Lk. 10:13-15)

Fourth, if they persist in their rejection we must make it clear they are not rejecting us, but God -- who will bring them to judgment for their sins. (Lk. 10:11-16) We need to be sure we "speak the truth in love" (Eph. 4:15) so that our message is not needlessly harsh. But in the face of determined rejection, there must be a clear warning of the consequences.

Fifth, we need to move ahead to our next assignment in God's harvest field. This is not an arbitrary decision. We can expect God to lead us onward.

Jesus Predicted Exponential Growth

Knowing that resistant harvest fields lie ahead should not detract from the truth of God's declaration that the "fields are white unto harvest." Those who may not respond must not diminish our expectation of the numbers who *will* respond.

Jesus described his life and ministry as that of a "mustard seed" or a "pinch of yeast put into a batch of flour." (Matt. 13:31-33) These are illustrations of exponential growth.

Indeed, Jesus' ministry began in a small, out-of-the-way district, with a tiny following of disciples, in a very big world. Yet Jesus told his disciples that his message would fill the earth. (Matt. 24:14)

In the parable of the four types of soil, Jesus says that good spiritual ground will produce ..."a crop — some thirty, some sixty, some a hundred times what was sown." (Mk. 4:20) Can you imagine harvesting a "hundred times what was sown"? Jesus is not expecting the church to have a good harvest, but rather an *explosive* harvest.

In another parable, Jesus speaks of the kingdom's growth as being irresistible:

> And He said, "So is the kingdom of God, as if a man should cast seed into the ground; and should sleep, and rise night and day, and <u>the seed should spring up and grow, he knows not how</u>. For the earth brings out fruit of itself, first the blade, then the ear, after that the full grain in the ear. But when the fruit has been brought out, immediately he puts in the sickle, because the harvest has come."(Mk. 4:26-29, Matt. 13:24-30)

From this parable we can see that the early church is "the blade," or the early stage of kingdom growth. In later generations of the church, the Spirit of God would produce the "head" (an expanded level of kingdom growth). Then, toward the end of this harvesting age, the Holy Spirit would bring forth the "full grain in the head" – the fullest manifestation of the kingdom through the church. (Mk. 4:28-32)

All 2000 years of church history have been building to this point in time. Jesus knew the gospel would begin small and insignificant in the eyes of the world, but would grow until it no longer could be ignored. (Mk. 4 :32)

The Fulfillment Of Jesus' Prediction

Let's compare the church's growth with the world's population growth. The world's population has increased at a staggering rate. At the time of Christ's birth, the population of the world was estimated to be less than 300 million people. By 1804 A.D. the population had grown to one billion people. By 2012 A.D. it had ballooned to seven billion people.
It took until 1804 for the world to reach its first billion people.

72

It has only taken 208 years to jump from that to 7 billion people. Estimates put us at 9 billion people within the next 34 years.

In comparison with the stunning growth of the world's

World Population Growth:
Material from Wikipedia on World Population
(in billions)

1804	1927	1960	1974	1987	1999	2012	2027	2046
1	2	3	4	5	6	7	8 (est.)	9 (est.)

population, what has the church's growth looked like? The Late Dr. Ralph Winters of the U.S. Center of World Missions, and former editor of their magazine *Mission Frontiers,* did a paper some years ago that provides the surprising answer.

Dr. Winters' report states that in 100 A.D. there was only one believer for every 360 people in the world. By 1000 A.D. there was one believer for every 270 people in the world. By 1500 A.D. there was one believer for every 85 people in the world. By 1900 A.D. there was one believer for every 13 people in the world. By 2010 there was one believer for every 7.3 people in the world. [vi]

A.D. 100	A.D. 1000	A.D. 1500	A.D. 1900	A.D. 1970	A.D. 2010
360:1	270:1	85:1	21:1	13:1	7.3:1

Several studies predict that by 2050 A.D. there will be around 3 billion Christians. If this is true, there will be one believer for every 3 people in the world.[vii]

Church growth over the last two millennia has been extraordinary. It is good to note that the church grew the most in the last 114 years, when the world's population was growing fastest.

God is fulfilling Jesus' promise of exponential kingdom growth into every nation of the world. But even more startling church growth is coming.

REVIEW OF CHAPTER FIVE

1. The definition of a spiritual harvest is the gathering of every man, woman, boy, girl, and creation itself, into the kingdom of God through faith in the message and work of Jesus Christ. God has always had it in his heart to bring back fallen man, and creation, into a redeemed relationship with himself. (Gen. 3:15, Gen. 12:3-4; Rom. 8:19-22)

2. The harvest is the paramount focus of God. It must be the primary focus of the church.

3. We do not have to pray for a riper harvest. It is fully ready. The real focus is to pray for ready harvesters.

4. There will be harvest fields that will be unbelieving and resistant to the gospel. Jesus does warn us of these, and instructs us how to deal with them. The important thing is to be sure we are in the field where God wants us, and to respond to it the way Jesus taught.

5. The spread of the church over the last two thousand years has proven that the church is fulfilling Jesus' prediction of exponential growth. It has become a world religion, flourishing in almost every culture. And it is far from done.

CHAPTER SIX

Preparing for the Harvest Wave

During my last pastorate, God blessed me with an intercessory team that met with me weekly, and prayed for me and for my ministry. During a Saturday prayer session, one of the intercessors had a mind's-eye vision from the Lord.

He saw a huge tsunami coming toward the church. The Lord spoke to him as he saw this great wave: "Get out your surfboard!"

This intercessor was never a surfer, but he understood what God was saying. God was ready to do a massive work around the world that would create a vast harvest wave of people, and the church had to get ready for it.

From what I understand about surfing, the idea is to catch the upswell of a strong wave at the right moment. If your timing is good, you can ride that wave all the way to the beach, accomplishing fancy maneuvers along the way.

You do not have to create the wave. You only have to ride it.

In Chapter Five, we defined the harvest and presented God's primary focus on harvesting the lost. We also looked at data showing how the Holy Spirit has been faithful to lead the church into becoming a worldwide harvesting force. Now we need to truly take stock of the size of the coming harvest wave – it will be overwhelming -- and there is an urgency to get ready for it.

In this chapter, and those following, we will explore three scripture passages to see how God by his Spirit will unleash this wave.

A Final, Intense Outpouring

The prophet Joel predicted a worldwide ongoing "outpouring" of the Holy Spirit through the age of harvest:

> And afterward, I will pour out my Spirit on all people. Your sons and daughters will prophesy, your old men will dream dreams, your young men will see visions. Even on my servants, both men and women, I will pour out my Spirit in those days. I will show wonders in the heavens and on the earth, blood and fire and billows of smoke. The sun will be turned to darkness and the moon to blood before the coming of the great and dreadful day of the Lord. And everyone who calls on the name of the Lord will be saved..." (Joel 2:28-32 NIV)

This outpouring was to be marked by two powerful spiritual movements, at its beginning and at its end. A careful study of Joel's prediction discloses these two spiritual outpourings, first presented by Dr. David Wesley Myland in a 1910 treatise entitled "The Latter Rain Pentecost." [viii]

Dr. Myland pointed out that Peter in his Pentecost sermon only quotes Joel 2:28-32 in referring to the first great outpouring of God's Spirit. Myland insists that we must consider the added study of Joel 2:23-27 as central to understanding the prophecy.

78

The Context For The Latter Rain

Israel had sinned against the Lord. God had judged Israel with a drought, and with a plague of locusts that destroyed the nation's crops. God ordained Joel to call the people to turn their hearts back to obedience, so his judgments could be removed.

In verse 18 of Joel 2, the prophet indicates that after bringing great devastation upon sinning Israel, God was filled with mercy and forgiveness. He spoke comfort to the devastated nation and was determined to restore it.

God had decided to remove Israel's shame from before the nations (vs.19) and to restore the rain cycle so his people could once again enjoy a harvest of wine and grain. He declared that he would drive off the devouring locust army and destroy it. (vs. 20)

Joel then predicted that after the Lord removed his judgments, he would restore his presence. He would pour out his Holy Spirit on Israel and draw them close to himself. (vs. 28-29) The signs for this would be the people prophesying God's word and receiving divine communication through dreams.

Dr. Myland held that in carrying this prophecy forward to the age of the church, you cannot arbitrarily separate God's deliverance and the outpouring of his Spirit. They are intertwined.

In Joel 2: 23, the prophet refers to the restoration of the rain cycle to the land. The Palestinian rain cycle is initiated by an "early rain," called the "Yarah Rain." This falls between

September 15 and November 15, preparing the ground for plowing and the planting of seed.

The rain cycle concludes with the "latter rain," called the "Malqosh Rain." This falls between March 15 and May 15, and matures the crops for harvest.

This restoration of rain was part of a pair of divine blessings. The first blessing was the removal of judgment; the second was the restoring of God's presence among his people.

In vs. 28 of the second chapter of Joel, the prophet declares "… and it shall come to pass afterwards…." This phrase is not found in Peter's Pentecost message. Peter uses the phrase "…and it shall come to pass in the last days, says the Lord." (Acts 2:17)

Some bible teachers have felt Peter simply misquoted Joel, but I do not think that is the case. I believe the Holy Spirit inspired Peter to change the phrase.

Joel's phrase indicates that the blessing of God's restored presence would come after the salvation of the nation from God's devastating judgments. Peter's phrase takes Joel's prophetic promise out of the immediate context of the 8th century B.C. and places it in the last days.

Peter gives Joel's prophecy a deeper, greater fulfillment in the future. But in Peter's message we are not dealing with a physical restoration of Israel, but with a spiritual restoration of that nation. Both promises of national salvation and empowerment found in Joel's prophecy are brought forward to Peter's day.

Here Israel's salvation was to turn into a universal salvation for all nations. Joel is promising that the presence of the Lord will come upon "all flesh" after spiritual salvation has come to all who receive Jesus as their savior. The evidence of this great salvation and empowerment was to be the gifting of new languages and prophecy – which indeed were present on the day of Pentecost.

Both Joel and Peter use the phrase "pour forth," which means to "gush or shed." Both identify the coming of the Holy Spirit as a spiritual "gushing or pouring" rain.

Once we understand that both Israel's salvation and empowerment speak to the future, we gain a better understand of the Holy Spirit's outpouring during the last days.

Remember that the Lord deliberately sent the outpouring of the Holy Spirit at the time of the Jewish Feast of Pentecost. There is no mistaking God's prophetic meaning in his timing.

Clearly, this first outpouring of the Holy Spirit initiated the *continuous* outpouring of the Spirit throughout the present age of harvest. (Acts 2:39)

If Pentecost was the celebration of first fruits or the "yarah rain" to initiate the harvest, then there will be a final or "malqosh rain" to bring the full harvest to readiness.

The Last Great Outpouring

Having considered both Joel's and Peter's prophecies, we need to grasp the impact of a final great outpouring of the Holy Spirit on the end-times harvest. This final outpouring will "bring the harvest to full readiness" -- which was the purpose of the "latter rain" in the Palestinian rain cycle.

According to Jesus, the outpouring of the Spirit was to empower the church to be God's witness to all nations. (Acts 1:8) It did. The Holy Spirit took discouraged and fearful disciples and turned them into a powerhouse for the kingdom of God.

It is estimated that the church grew to about 20,000 believers within its first decade. Paul declared that the gospel had been carried forth to the known world before his death. (Col. 1:6) The initial outpouring of the Holy Spirit caused the church to grow from 120 believers to tens of thousands of believers within 30 years of the event.

Imagine what will happen when the greater outpouring of the Holy Spirit falls on a world church – numbering over 2 billion people -- that is now in almost every nation and people group!

In Book Two of this series we will go into more depth about what I see as the beginning of this second great outpouring. I will deal with the history of the church over the last two hundred years, tracking Spirit-inspired revival and reformation that is becoming a worldwide phenomenon.

I believe the day is coming when we will see the phenomena of Acts 2 happening in every nation and city, stirring God's people to great acts of faith.

REVIEW OF CHAPTER SIX

1. The church must be poised to surf the coming harvest wave. We must grasp its vast size, and the speed at which it will arrive. We must gain a sense of urgency so that ripe and ready people in this wave will not be lost to the kingdom of God.

2. In Joel 2:23-32 the prophet teaches that a mighty second outpouring of the Holy Spirit is coming in the last days, one that will bring the great harvest to readiness. This unprecedented worldwide outpouring will awaken the church and empower it to effectively reach those God has shaken into readiness to receive him.

CHAPTER SEVEN

A Continuous Harvest

As I have mentioned, I had the privilege of participating in the Jesus Movement of the late 1960s and early 1970s. I remember how it seemed so easy for the kids at our commune house, and even members at our church, to find people eager to receive Christ as their savior.

I recall showing up for an evening meeting at the commune house to discover over 300 people trying to get in, some even leaning through the windows to hear the worship and teaching. At times we saw weekly -- if not daily -- decisions being made for the Lord. We were continually baptizing people, so much so that it became a routine experience.

Then the pace changed. Our evangelism ride went from cruise control to low gear, and finally to stop-and-go. Sadly, we realized the movement was coming to a close. But while it lasted, it was thrilling.

As extraordinary as that was, it won't compare to the rush of evangelism that God will release in the last days. One major characteristic of the final wave of harvest will be continuous sowing and reaping, bringing new believers into the Kingdom of God. As this age finishes, we will see an immediate, sustained response to the proclamation of the gospel.

This insight of a continuous harvest is found in Amos 9:11-13 (NIV).

"In that day I will restore David's fallen shelter — I will repair its broken walls and restore its ruins — and will rebuild it as it used to be, so that they may possess the remnant of Edom and all the nations that bear my name," ..... "The days are coming," declares the Lord, "when the reaper will be overtaken by the plowman and the planter by the one treading grapes."

Salvation By Faith And Grace Alone

The context of this passage is Amos prophesying the destruction of Israel's ten northern tribes, which happened during the 7th century B.C. And yet as the prophecy closes in Chapter 9, Amos offers a gleam of hope: There will come a day when God will restore Israel to its land, and remove his judgment. God promises that Israel will be used to rebuild God's Kingdom through a descendant of David, who will rule the nations.

This echoes the Lord's promise in 2 Sam. 7:16-18, that one of David's descendants would save his people and usher in divine kingdom rule over the nations. (Lk. 1:69-70; Rom. 15:12)

But when Israel rejected its Messiah, the Jews lost the right to represent the kingdom of God to the world. (Matt. 21:43) Instead, Jesus -- a descendant of David (Lk. 1:32) -- would raise up the church for that work.

This prediction of the "Tabernacle of David" (the coming messianic kingdom of God) is quoted by Jesus' half brother James in Acts 15, at the Jerusalem conference.

The focus of this conference was not about the success of God's Kingdom spreading to the world. Rather, it was about how that gospel would be preached. Would new converts have to keep the law and follow Jewish religious practices as part of their justification in receiving Christ as their savior?

No, James had come to understand – with the help of the Holy Spirit – that Amos' prophecy referred to God's salvation by grace and faith alone.

"David's tent," or tabernacle, was not just an allusion to the restored government of David, but also to his type of worship.

David early in his reign so deeply wanted the presence of God in his new capital of Jerusalem that he literally brought up the Ark of the Covenant by itself from the tabernacle, and placed it in a special tent. (1 Chron.16)

What David did was a violation of the Lord's commands to Moses about the treatment of the tabernacle. David did not bring the whole tabernacle of Moses from Shiloh, as he should have. He took only the Ark of the Covenant – out of a hungry heart for God's presence.

Astonishingly, after a limited correction God did not stop David. Instead, God was merciful and blessed David, because of David's heart attitude.

David went on to develop a form of worship never practiced in the Tabernacle of Moses. He set up continuous passionate prophetic singing and worship in front of the tent containing only the Ark. David wrote many worship songs, and sponsored others to be sung there. (1 Chronicles 15; 25:1-3) Eventually his new form of worship was carried into Solomon's temple.

James recognized the extraordinary expression of mercy and grace that God had extended toward David. By the help of the Holy Spirit, James saw God's response to David as a parallel to what God was doing in Paul's and Barnabas' ministry to the Gentiles.

James caught the meaning of Amos' Chapter 9, pointing to a time in the future when the Lord would again raise up Davidic worship, and attitudes toward God, based on mercy and grace, not on law.

Continuous Harvesting And Reaping

There is more in Amos than what James singled out.

The two verses James quotes in Amos 9:11-12 cannot be separated from the rest of the verses that finish the chapter. (vss.13-15) Understanding this, we see that when David's Tent is re-established there will come a supernatural harvest – to occur when Israel will never be removed from its land again.

James shows that verses 11 and 12 speak to the last days -- and so does the rest of the chapter.

> "The days are coming," declares the Lord, 'when the reaper will be overtaken by the plowman and the planter by the one treading grapes. New wine will drip from the mountains and flow from all the hills, and I will bring my people Israel back from exile. They will rebuild the ruined cities and live in them. They will plant vineyards and drink their wine; they will make gardens and eat their fruit. I will plant Israel in

their own land, never again to be uprooted from the land I have given them,' says the Lord your God." (Amos 9:13-15)

We have noted that Israel was destroyed as a nation in 70 A.D., and was not restored as a nation until 1948. Thus the prophecy would have to refer to a time *after* 1948, since most conservative Bible teachers believe Israel is back on its land to stay.

James makes it clear that verses 11 and 12 include the gentile church and its end-time mission to the nations. The subsequent agricultural reference in vs. 13 must refer to the church also. It is physically impossible to sow and reap at the same time. So we have a prophetic picture of a continuous spiritual harvest that will be experienced by the end-times church.

Verse 13 also includes a picture of an overflowing harvest of grapes "melting the hills." Mountains and hills often represent nations or kingdoms. (Isa. 2:2; Mich. 4:1; Rev. 17:9) This passage then pictures an overflowing, abundant, continuous harvest that will come when David's Tent (true grace-based worship and salvation through Jesus Christ) is proclaimed by the church at the end of the age of harvest. (Jn. 4:23-24)

Preparing For A Spiritual Flash Flood

It may be hard to visualize such a fruitful future for the church, but we must take God at his word. As I considered this passage, I felt that the Lord gave me a picture of someone standing in a dry riverbed in a desert area. Everything looked completely barren and arid. But there was a sign posted nearby: "Watch out for flash floods!"

A flash flood can overwhelm someone standing in a dry riverbed before they have time to run to safety. I believe God's word is warning us that he is going to produce an environment in the world at the end of time that will bring a sudden and overwhelming flood of people ready to receive the gospel.

God posted the warning signs centuries ago. Will we be caught unprepared?

REVIEW OF CHAPTER SEVEN

1. The controversy that the Apostles Paul and Barnabas stirred up in the early church over salvation by faith alone brought a unique insight into the coming climax of the age of the harvest. James the brother of Jesus was led by the Holy Spirit to recognize the prophecy of Amos as referring to a time when living by the law will give way to all being justified by faith in what Jesus Christ accomplished for us on the cross.

2. Being alerted to Amos 9's implications for the end-times church, we can look at the full context of that chapter to discover there will be a "continuous harvest" of ready people. This will come through the church reaching every nation and people group in fulfillment of the great commission. As Israel resumes its nationhood, the Holy Spirit will produce such a ripe field that the church will experience a continuous harvest. The church must be ready to disciple this vast influx.

CHAPTER EIGHT

The Jewish Harvest Wave

Israel always seems to be in the news -- usually at the center of controversy. Remarkably, it is one of the few ancient civilizations that has had most of its original land restored. For such a small nation, it has an incredible impact on world stability.

Scripture is clear that God planned – millennia ago -- to restore Israel. Moreover, its restoration was to be a signal, telling the church and the world to prepare for Jesus' second coming. Let's turn to Isaiah 49. Here we see that at the end of this age, there will be an unprecedented move of God among Jewish people.

There are four passages in the Book of Isaiah referred to as "songs of the servant," which point to the coming Messiah. These passages are found in Isaiah 42:1-4; 49:1-11 ; 50:4-9 and 52:13 - 53:12.

I want to look specifically at the servant song found in Isaiah 49. The Lord's servant in this song is given the assignment of restoring captured Israel, and going as a light to the gentile nations. (Isa. 49:6) Luke's gospel directly quotes this verse (Luke 2:32), confirming that this servant is Jesus Christ in his first coming.

Almost always when Messiah is spoken of as a "light" to the nations, the reference is to the gospel work of Jesus through his church.

This song shows that the messianic servant will not come as the military leader that the Jews of the 1st century were expecting. Instead, he will come as a gentle, redemptive messenger. (Isa. 42: 3; Isa. 49:4, 7a; Isa. 53:1-12)

He will be despised by his people, yet Gentile kings will recognize who he is, and rise in respect and worship of God because of him. (49:7)

Isaiah 49:8 declares that at the coming of this servant there will be a time of salvation for God's people and the world. Paul quotes verse eight in 2 Cor.6:2, saying "now is the acceptable time of salvation."

The servant is coming to restore all people to a righteous relationship with the Lord. He will tell "spiritual" prisoners to leave their prisons and step out of the darkness, to begin walking the "highway of redemption." (Isa. 49:11 GNB)

This salvation highway, for both Jew and Gentile, will be used to bring Israel's children home from around the world.

Isaiah 49:12 introduces one of the most exciting aspects of this song. The scene shifts to the future, in which Israel -- newly released from captivity -- is returning to the destroyed nation. The former captives are grieving the destruction of their nation; they are saying God has forsaken them, and forgotten them. (49:14) But Jehovah assures them that he never forgot them.

The Lord asks, "How could a mother forget her nursing child?" Israel has been engraved on the palm of God's hand for a continuous reminder of his love, and of his covenant with their forefathers. (Rom. 11:28)

Today, dating from 1948, Israel is reviving as a nation – one that was only a memory for almost 2,000 years. Its history is one of persecution, captivity, and death. But over the last seven decades we have watched Israel reassert itself.

No, God has not forgotten this people.

Picking up the story in verse 18 of Isaiah 49, we see something catching the eye of discouraged Israel: Children of various ages are quickly making their way toward the exiles, who are standing among the ruins of Jerusalem.

These children have come "from afar -- from every direction of the earth." (49:12, 17) As they approach, the Lord breaks into joyful singing, purposing to comfort his afflicted people. As Israel's "children from the nations" run toward the ruined city, God is forcing those who enslaved Israel to release it.

It is almost like an exorcism, through which those who had conquered sinful Israel are now by grace being driven away by God. (49:17, 24-25) In this national deliverance Jehovah is displaying to "all flesh" (the world) his amazing love for this people, showing how he is their mighty redeemer. (vs. 26)

While the children run toward the stunned former captives, God announces that they are "wedding ornaments" for Israel to wear on its future wedding dress. (vs.18) Widowed Israel, bereft of its children, desolate and homeless for so long, suddenly learns that God will marry her again.

Here is a clear picture of Israel's first-fruits harvest, as seen in Revelation 7, preparing the nation for its eventual salvation and inclusion into the Body of Christ. I encourage you to see Appendix One for a better understanding of the end-times harvest among the Jewish people.

Remember: The servant in the song is Jesus. There can only be one "marriage covenant" that God will enter into with Israel, as spoken of in Ezek. 34:23-25, 36:24-29 and Jer. 31:31-34. It is the new covenant in Jesus' blood, with Israel being joined to the "Bride of Christ." (Matt. 26:28; Rev. 21:9)

The returning children shout to the exiles, "There are too many returning children to live in this narrow, small place." (vs.19) What a statement for a discouraged nation to hear! Israel is overwhelmed with the sudden turn of events. "Who birthed these children?" Israel asks. "My children were killed and taken away. I did not birth these. And who raised them? Where did they come from?" (49:21)

Jehovah does not answer the question; instead he speaks to the future. He tells Israel that he will "signal to the Gentile nations" to bring all their scattered children home.

The "signal" or "banner" referenced here is a military standard that shows soldiers where to rally on the battlefield. Gentile leaders will recognize the signal, and will respond to God's call to bring Israel's children home.

Notice the picture of tenderness as these national leaders carry Israel's children home on their shoulders, and in their bosom, like spiritual parents. (49:22-23) This is the Gentile church being used to draw Jewish people back to him. It fulfills the dream of the Apostle Paul, who prayed that his ministry to the Gentiles would prompt his people to turn to their true Messiah:

> I say then, Did they [Israel] stumble that they
> might fall? God forbid: but by their fall salvation
> is come unto the Gentiles, to provoke them to

jealousy. Now if their fall, is the riches of the world, and their loss the riches of the Gentiles; how much more their fullness?" But I speak to you that are Gentiles. Inasmuch then as I am an apostle of the Gentiles, I glorify my ministry; if by any means I may provoke to jealousy them that are my flesh, and may save some of them. For if the casting away of them is the reconciling of the world, what shall the receiving of them be, but life from the dead?" (Rom. 11:11-15)

Isaiah is watching Paul's spiritual dream come true at the end of time. The prophet is depicting a modern exodus that will shock the land of Israel.

Remember, Isaiah 49 is speaking of the "suffering messiah" and not the "ruling messiah." Consequently, we are not looking at the millennial reign of Christ, but at the end of this age.

What is so exciting is the surge in returning Messianic Jews impacting the nation with a population problem, and surprising a watching world.

There is much pain yet to come to natural Israel -- but as God's church loves it, and brings home its saved and transformed children, God will set up the nation for the day when all Israel will embrace its true Messiah. (Zech.12)

Israel's Help In The Coming Harvest

This last-days move of God among the Jewish people will release a wave of dynamic harvest workers.

Paul says that as Israel begins to come back to the Lord, it will be an incredible testimony to the world of God's resurrection power. (Rom. 11:15) Paul is declaring that the restoration of Israel will be one of the greatest demonstrations of the might of Jesus Christ to save.

In Isaiah 49 we see a Jewish harvest wave that will add to the worldwide wave. As Jewish people begin to identify with their Messiah, Yeshua (Jesus), and begin to proclaim the gospel, they will have a profound impact.

Our job is to stay spiritually awake, and be prepared. You can't swim out to surf a wave that is already starting to crest. You have to be in place, and ready for it.

This is our challenge – to believe what scripture is telling us, and allow the Holy Spirit to position us for what is to come.

REVIEW OF CHAPTER EIGHT

1. One of the four messianic servant songs in the book of Isaiah is Isaiah 49 -- often quoted in the New Testament to reveal Jesus Christ as the coming Messiah. These New Testament verses help us interpret Isaiah 49 as speaking to the work of the church in evangelizing both the Gentile nations and Israel in the last days. (Isa. 49:6 - Lk. 2:32; Isa. 49:8 – 2 Cor.6:2; Isa. 49:24 - Matt. 12:29)

2. God will increasingly empower the Gentile church to draw hundreds of thousands of Jewish people to faith in Christ. Christian groups and national leaders will participate in helping saved Jewish people return to Israel to spark a national revival of faith in Jesus as Messiah. This "first fruits" movement of Israel will become a powerful resurrection witness to a watching world. (Rev. 14:4b; Rom.11: 15)

PART THREE
God's End-time Audacity

I remember a time when I felt that the miracles of the Old Testament seemed to be so much more impressive than those seen in the gospels and the Book of Acts. I always thought that the Old Covenant seemed more dynamic than the New Covenant, aside from the story of the Resurrection, with accounts of "seas splitting apart" and "fire falling from heaven" and the "sun standing still."

But as the Lord led me in a fresh study through the Book of Revelation, it was as if he pulled back spiritual curtains, revealing that some of his greatest miracles are yet in store.

God is going to end the last-days harvest season with "divine audacity." The word audacity means "extremely bold or daring; brave, fearless; unrestrained by existing ideas." [ix]

Let me give you an example of God increasing his audacious witness through the Holy Spirit in the outreach of the church.

For 1,200 years, Muslim culture has been notoriously resistant to the gospel. Nevertheless, in the last decade the mission organization of City Team Ministries launched a vigorous church planting strategy among Muslim populations.

God surprised City Team with miraculous support. Whole mosques and entire villages of Islamic believers have begun to experience conversions through divine dreams and angelic visitations.

Jerry Trousdale, City Team Director of International Ministries, wrote:

> In the last seven years, we have had a chance to hear hundreds of stories … about the dreams that God is using to reach Muslim people … former Muslim leaders who are now making disciples and planting churches. About 40 percent reported a dream or vision of Jesus that prompted them to begin a search to know more about Isa al Masih (Jesus the Messiah)"[x]

Trousdale estimates that over a million Muslims are being converted to Christ each year. [xi] This is just one of many audacious works that God is doing already, works I will cover further in Book Three of this series.

In this next section I want to present the biblical foundation for the growing audacity of God. It is not my purpose to build graphs or prophetic charts to explain the deep mysteries of the book of Revelation. Rather, I want you to look through the telescope of scripture toward where God is taking us as a witnessing/harvesting church.

We must become comfortable with the idea that God is going to increasingly do audacious works, and that he wants us to develop audacious faith he can work through. We must believe he will give us a miraculous witness to whole people groups and nations. We must stir up our faith to believe beyond our ability. We must not limit what God will call on us to accomplish as we move toward the close of the age.

CHAPTER NINE

God's Audacious Suffering Love

In 1956, five young missionaries agreed to make contact with the Huraorani tribe in eastern Ecuador – a tribe that had never been reached with the gospel. The surrounding tribes called the Huraorani "auca": *savage*. They were extremely dangerous.

Despite the risk, the five missionaries journeyed to the Huraorani's territory, attempting an outreach. The effort was dubbed "Operation Auca." Sadly, it was well named. The tribe responded by killing every one of the young men.

A year after the massacre, the wife of one of the five, Elizabeth Elliot, determined to keep trying to get through to this tribe for Christ. It was a courageous step of faith – and it succeeded. Within two years of her husband's death, Elizabeth Elliot had not only brought the gospel to the Huraorani, but had led to Christ the very man who murdered her husband Jim.

Jim's death had moved Elizabeth Elliot to a higher commitment of service to the Lord. She went on to write 20 books, and shared her husband's story with hundreds of thousands of people. Though Jim and his companions lost their own lives, through Elizabeth's work they inspired new mission volunteers to live "sold-out" lives for Christ.

God's Sacrificial Love

How amazing is God's love for us! His love for lost humanity has caused him to be willing to allow his spiritual sons and daughters to suffer and even die to reveal it.

In Revelation 7:9-17 we find an incalculable number of people standing before the throne of God, arrayed in white robes. They have come out of a time of great suffering – the tribulation -- at the hands of Antichrist. They represent every language, tribe, and nation. They have stood the test and won the victory in Christ.

In Revelation 6 we see the opening of the fifth seal, with the cry of the martyrs asking God to avenge their blood on the forces of Antichrist. (Rev. 6:9-10) God tells them to wait a short while longer, because he is going to give the world a little more time to decide for Christ – even though further martyrdom will take place.

As I read these passages, the Lord impressed on my heart his willingness to "spend" the lives of his precious saints to reach the most hard-hearted and violent sinners.

It might seem to us that martyrdom and the suffering of God's people would be something God would seek to avoid. Yet, God is willing to call his people to endure such trials.

This whole idea of suffering for Jesus seems to fly in the face of much of the popular preaching we hear today. Many congregations are being told the Christian life is the path to self-fulfillment and to gaining whatever we need.

It is true that God will take care of his people's needs, and that serving the Lord will bring fulfillment of our life's purpose. But trusting Christ as our savior does not ensure pain-free living.

Life brings challenges. God is there to help us through them – not always to get us out of them. The plain truth is that we grow in times of trials more than we do in times of blessings.

We need both.

Too often, mainstream preaching glosses over our position as God's bondservants, to be used as best benefits his kingdom.

Paul says we are "slaves of Christ" who have been bought by his blood. (1 Cor. 7:23) Slaves do not direct their own lives; they do the bidding of their master. And because of God's great love for the lost, some of us will be assigned to reach out to lost people like the Huraorani.

Peter writes –

> It was to this that God called you, for Christ himself suffered for you and left you an example, so that you would follow in his steps."
> (1 Pet. 2:21)

Few of us are inclined to volunteer for redemptive suffering. Yet, if we serve the Lord it will come in some form. (2 Tim. 3:12) We need to accept this truth, and remember that no one can face such trials in their own strength. We must lean into the Holy Spirit, and keep close fellowship with those who will stand with us in our time of struggle and pain.
(2 Cor.1:4-5; Heb. 10:24-25)

Even more, we must remember to bless God in such times. James, the brother of Jesus, exhorts us to "count it all joy" when we come into trials and suffering, knowing that God is building us into the persons he wants us to be. (James 1:2-3)

Recently I read a report of over a million Christians in war-torn Iraq, seeking to flee persecution. Many were given an ultimatum: Leave their homes within two days, or be killed. Many lost their lives in this cruel persecution. Martyrdom is very much a reality in our day and age.

Purpose Of Redemptive Suffering

As I have reflected on God's audacity in reaching out to a lost world through times of great suffering on the part of his people, I have seen two important spiritual facts. The first is that such sacrifice shows the great love God has for the lost. The second is the purifying work and glory that such suffering will produce in the church.

No one questions the fact of God's great love in the sacrifice of his only son as a demonstration of his love for us. (Rom. 5:8) The continued suffering of God's people in Jesus' redemptive work is an extension of that amazing love. (Col. 1:24)

But I want to focus our attention on this second fact. Scripture promises that the day will come when the Lord will "present to himself a church without spot or wrinkle . . . holy and without blemish." (Eph. 5:27) When God's people offer themselves on the altar of sacrifice (Rom. 12:1) with a truly surrendered heart to God, it purifies them of sinful tendencies and builds into them the ways and thinking of the new man in Christ. (Col. 3:9; Eph. 4:22)

Peter states that those who have suffered for the cause of Christ in the flesh find the power of sin broken more and more in their life. (1 Pet. 4:1)

I am not saying that redemptive suffering makes a believer perfect; but it does move them to greater spiritual maturity. The end-time church generation will suffer more than any other for the cause of Christ. In light of this, clearly that generation will manifest the greatest maturity and holy living of any in the church age. I can see how Isaiah can say of the end-time church:

> Arise, shine; for thy light is come, and the glory of Jehovah is risen upon you . . . . Jehovah will arise upon you, and his glory shall be seen upon you. And nations shall come to your light, and kings to the brightness of your rising. (Isa. 60:1-2)

Haggai is correct: The end-time church (the restored temple) will be filled with the glory of the Lord that the nations will see.

An Uncountable Harvest
(The Impact of Redemptive Love on the Harvest)

So, will the audacious, suffering love of God through his people have an impact on the coming harvest?

Review again Revelation 7:9. Listen to how the Apostle John describes this group of suffering saints: "...there was a large crowd that *no one was able to count!*" The number of people coming out of this three-and-a-half year period of time -- from every language, nation, and tribe -- was beyond reckoning.

The suffering under Antichrist will not frustrate the harvest of the church. Instead, we see the church rising up and being victorious through it all. In this passage we find the dramatic fulfillment of Jesus' prophecy of the gospel reaching every nation. (Matt. 24:14). Not even Antichrist can stop it.

No Sacrifice For Christ Will Be In Vain

Such suffering and injustice may seem very wrong. It is natural for us to want God to bring deliverance in circumstances like that. But as his servants, we must embrace the fact that he did not spare his only begotten son. (Rom. 8:32) Why then would we feel he should not spend our lives for the sake of the gospel?

Yet, God will mark and remember any sacrifice we make for his Kingdom. (Heb. 6:10) Scripture declares, "precious in the sight of the Lord is the death of his saints." (Ps. 116:15)

God loves us deeply and does not spend our lives carelessly. In reviewing Hebrews 11, often called "the faith chapter," we see that God decides what will glorify his name most -- our deliverance, or our sacrifice. (Heb. 11:32-38) If God does decide to allow us to enter times of suffering for his name's sake, he will give us the strength to face it. Ultimately our attitude must reflect what the Apostle Paul wrote –

> My deep desire and hope is that I shall never fail in my duty, but that at all times, and especially right now, I shall be full of courage, so that with my whole being I shall bring honor to Christ, whether I live or die. (Phil. 1:20 GNB)

It is written about Paul and Barnabas that, as they went about confirming and strengthening their new disciples and churches, they taught them:

> "... to continue in the faith, and that we must through much tribulation enter into the kingdom of God." (Acts 14:22)

Are we to teach any less as we see the close of this age coming? I am not trying to be negative, but the future is going to call for great courage and faith. Don't cheat God's people. Let them know the truth and prepare them for what lies ahead. We must all pick up our cross and follow him wherever he leads us.

"Then Jesus told his disciples, 'If anyone would come after me, let him deny himself and take up his cross and follow me. For whoever would save his life will lose it, but whoever loses his life for my sake will find it.'" (Matt. 16:24-25)

REVIEW OF CHAPTER NINE

1. In the first illustration of God's extravagant love in Revelation 7, we see his willingness to spend the lives of his precious saints to win the hardest of sinners. As believers, we must have a servant heart that allows God to spend our lives as he sees fit.

2. In Revelation 7:9-17 we see that God's audacious redemptive love will cause an uncountable number of people to be saved and enter into his Kingdom. Antichrist will not be able to stop the great harvest, despite his all-out persecution of the church.

Chapter Ten

The Two Witnesses

"Won't someone shut those two up!" shouted the Supreme Leader. "The whole world tunes in every day to listen to them. I am getting tired of the impact their preaching is having. Their illegal church is growing, and even whole cities are converting to their message. I will not stand for it!"

"But Your Illuminance," came the trembling reply, "many have tried and failed. It does not end well for those who make the attempt."

"Well, my power is growing -- and soon I myself will confront them! They will fall, I promise you that!"

This is how I envision Antichrist responding to the preaching of the two witnesses the Apostle John writes about in Revelation 11.

Those amazing prophetic leaders are our next illustration of how God is going to reveal his audacious love for his church in its most difficult time.

Revelation 11:1-12 starts with John being given a rod to measure the temple of God, its altar, and the worshippers within it during the tribulation period. Here Jesus is not speaking to John about a physical temple, but about the church (1 Cor. 3:16). This will be the only temple God will inhabit in the last days. [xii]

Examples of prophetic measuring found in scripture have to do with divine evaluation of spiritual conditions, and with

God's commitment to restore his people.

In Ezekiel 40 we find the prophet watching as an angel measures the "restored temple" of God at the end of time. Again, in Revelation 21:15 we find an angel measuring the new eternal city of Jerusalem. In Zechariah 4:10 we also find a reference to Prince Zerubbabel having a "plumb-line in his hands" as he was sent to rebuild the temple after 70 years of national captivity.

I believe that in tying the prophetic measuring of the church to the two witnesses in Revelation 11, the Lord is pointing to them as a key way he will both build up the church and sustain it during this tumultuous episode.

A Worldwide Witness

The reference to the "Holy City" cites Jerusalem as the place for the climactic confrontation between Antichrist and God's Two Witnesses. In verse 3, John introduces the two prophets that God will raise up to confront the growing message and power of Antichrist. Their witness will come in the last three and half years of this age.[xiii]

These two preachers will not only galvanize the church, but will provide a worldwide witness reaching millions with the gospel.

Zechariah 4

John's account bears a remarkable resemblance to a prophecy found in Zechariah 4. Zechariah, in tandem with the Prophet Haggai, had been sent by God to encourage the small remnant of Jews who returned to rebuild the temple in Jerusalem after 70 years of captivity in Babylon.

In Zechariah's message, he tried to encourage the people by calling on them to recognize what God was doing through his two anointed leaders (4:10-11). These leaders would provide "the spiritual light" (lampstand) for the people to know God's will in their time of rebuilding. (4:11-12).

Some Bible teachers believe the two leaders referred to in this post-exilic time were Prince Zerubbabel and the High Priest Joshua.

A Deeper Meaning

John sees a deeper fulfillment in Zechariah's message, just as the writer of Hebrews had seen a deeper meaning in Haggai's message. John turns Zechariah's prophecy into a double prophecy. He sees a greater future fulfillment in the two post-exilic leaders who will help build a different temple: the church at the end of this age.

The Ministry Of The Two Witnesses

John says these prophets will prophesy for 42 months during the time of the tribulation. Notice that they are clothed in sackcloth, which was an expression of sorrow and humiliation (Amos 8:10). The sackcloth speaks to the fact that they are calling for all to repent, to turn back to God, and turn away from Antichrist's message.

The fact that there are "two" witnesses is tied to the Old Covenant's demand that for any testimony to be considered valid, there had to be at least two witnesses (Deut. 19:15).

The Two Olive Trees

Both Zechariah and John describe the witnesses as "olive trees." Olive trees were the main source for lamp oil in Israel. Comparing these prophets to olive trees could only mean that they were the source of "fresh oil" (spiritual illumination and anointing). Oil in scripture is a symbol of the Holy Spirit's work of "equipping, empowering and inspiring" God's people. (2 Kings 9:6; Ps. 89:20; Matt. 25:1-5)

So, John sees that part of the ministry of these two witnesses is to supply spiritual inspiration, revelation, and strength to God's people during the time of tribulation (Jn. 5:35).

Zechariah gives the idea of the two olive trees a slightly different emphasis than does John. The prophet never refers to the two witnesses as lamps. Instead, he refers to them as the source of oil for a lamp that has seven bowls. The bowls contained the oil that fed each flame.

In Revelation 1:20 we are told that the seven churches John was addressing are called "lampstands." We are to understand, then, that the lampstands are God's people, who are to shine with God's life and glory in this dark world.

Zechariah highlights the two witnesses as inspiring and encouraging God's people to be a light of truth about God in the world. John's emphasis differs slightly, but is no less significant. John emphasizes the two witnesses themselves as being divine lights that in turn inspire the church to be a shining beacon to the world.

Satellite TV

One of the things many have noted in this passage is the world's constant awareness of what these two witnesses say and do. Clearly this passage anticipates the existence of worldwide communications – something that today we take for granted.

These witnesses have a constant global audience of those who love them, and those who hate them. Neither Zechariah or John could have envisioned the internet or satellite television – but conceptually, they were in fact "early adopters."

Divine Superheroes

Reading the account of the two witnesses, I began to understand how the New Covenant will outshine the Old Covenant in the miraculous works God will perform before Jesus comes again.

Look carefully at how God is going to empower these two prophets: They will be able to destroy their enemies with fire. They will be able to stop the rain over nations. They will be able to make lakes and water sources undrinkable. They will be able to send plagues on cities, or entire world regions.

Can you recognize any of these powers in other Biblical figures?

It was Elijah who called down fire on those sent to take him. (2 Kings 1:10)

It also was Elijah who stopped the rain over Israel for three years. (1 Kings 17)

It was Moses who turned the waters of the Nile into blood and brought plagues on Egypt. (Ex. 7-12

What we find in this passage of Revelation is a reprise of these amazing Old Testament stories for a worldwide audience on high-definition TV over a period of three and half years!

I do not doubt that fire will destroy those who try to hurt these leaders, but I feel the picture of fire coming from their mouths also has a figurative meaning (vs. 5). The prophet Jeremiah declared about God's word:

> My words are a powerful fire; they are a hammer that shatters rocks. (Jer 23:29)

We also find in Revelation 1:16 a reference to a "double-edged sword" coming out of Jesus' mouth. In another place, Jesus fights with the "sword of his mouth" and slays the wicked. (Rev. 2:16 and 19:21) These passages represent the power of God's word spoken through Jesus and his prophets.

So it will be with the two witnesses. They will have power to speak God's word like fire that will destroy and punish the evil machinations against them. But their word will also soften the hard hearts of sinners, opening them to receive the gospel.

A Spectacular Ending

As we discovered from our study of the uncountable saints in Revelation 7, the church will be harvesting vast numbers into the kingdom during this time of suffering. Every language and people group will have a growing church witness.

While martyrdom will dramatically increase, the two witnesses will inspire the church to win thousands upon thousands to faith in Christ.

People will recognize who has authority to affect the weather and punish nations. Remember, the power that Moses had to release plagues was directed at the supposed domains of each of Egypt's gods. Exodus portrays a "divine shoot-out" between Satan and God, with Jehovah showing his superior power.

With the two witnesses of Revelation, we see God displaying in an even mightier fashion his strong arm (Isa. 52:10). Only those who harden their hearts and refuse to believe will keep rejecting the gospel in the face of such epic evidence, and the witness of the church.

Like Jesus, these two prophets are given three and a half years to speak their message, during which time nothing can happen to them. Jesus would often say, "My time has not yet come." (Jn. 2:7; Matt. 26:18)

The preaching of the witnesses will be a "torment" for the wicked. For the church it will be a potent, sustaining word. The wicked will seethe, wanting to silence the troublesome gadflies – and some will try. The attacks will be futile. God will let nothing harm them before their appointed time.

Finally, as with Jesus, the hour will come for the two witnesses to die. The Evil One will slay them before a watching world, and all who trust Antichrist will rejoice.

Then God's audacity will crush the celebration.

Three days later the Lord will publicly resurrect them. There will be no mere rumor of their resurrection -- because the world will watch it live on satellite TV.

Now, whether this involves the rapture of the church, I am not sure. We do know that the "last trumpet" sounds in the next several verses (Rev. 11:15), which the Apostle Paul says is the sign of the rapture. (1 Cor.15:52)

But whether or not the resurrection of the two witnesses is part of the final rapture, John reports there will be worldwide holy fear, with people "giving glory to the God of Heaven" (vs.13).

God does not do drama for the sake of spectacle. He is going to audaciously force the world to acknowledge the stark choice between his salvation and the way of the Evil One.

And at that moment, some of the most recalcitrant sinners will at last bow their knee to God, and be saved.

REVIEW OF CHAPTER TEN

1. We see the measuring of the temple as a prophetic reference to the restoration of the end-times church, preparing it for the events of the last days. It appears that the two witnesses will be a source of renewal for the church.

2. The episode of the two witnesses is one of the most dramatic accounts in the Bible of God's outreach to a lost world. Several stories found in the Old Testament are amplified and brought together in the ministry of these two witnesses. God will allow them to enjoy worldwide power and communications for three and a half years. The church will be strengthened by them, and the wicked will be tormented by them. There will be few if any atheists left in the world. The two witnesses will be dramatically killed by Antichrist, and the wicked will savor a moment of victory – only to be forced to watch the witnesses' resurrection with shock and fear. Many will finally bow the knee and give glory to God.

CHAPTER ELEVEN

The Gospel Angel and Friends

When I was pastoring in Portland, Oregon, my wife and I built a friendship with the wife and pastor of the German Assembly of God church there. His wife told me several times, "I wish I could see an angel just once in my life!" She longed for this so fervently that I prayed God would one day allow her to experience an angelic visitation.

In the time of the great, final harvest, nobody on earth will be left wishing for an angelic visitation. Audaciously, God will see that the entire planet gets one – in triplicate.

Chapter 14 of Revelation gives an account of what some Bible teachers have called the "Gospel Angels." (Rev. 14:6-11) Interestingly, I find that when I mention "gospel angels" to Christians, often they know little if anything about them. Yet this has to be one the most fantastic episodes in scripture.

The Gospel Angels story begins with God assigning three angels the task of proclaiming the gospel to every nation and language, warning of coming judgment. It may be possible that some on earth will miss the message of the two witnesses -- but nobody will miss the messages of the three angels.

We have seen jet fighters overflying the opening ceremonies of major sporting events, like the Super Bowl – zooming with a deafening roar above a packed stadium. Those will seem like buzzing house flies compared with the global over-flights of the Gospel Angels.

Angel One

The message of the first angel has four parts: (1) Fear God and give him glory; (2) A proclamation of the eternal gospel to every nation, tribe, and tongue; (3) A warning of judgment coming on those who will not repent; (4) A call for all to worship he who made the heaven and the earth, sea, and fountains of waters.

The first angel expounds the most basic truth about Creator God. As Paul states, "every person is without excuse" to recognize that the universe has a designer (Rom. 1:19-20).

The core message of the first angel is simple: The Creator of all things sent his son, Jesus, to pay the price for our sins so we can repent and be restored to a relationship with him. The world must embrace the sacrifice of the Creator's son to avoid suffering the judgment of Satan and his followers.

Angel Two

The message of the second angel announces the collapse of the corrupt commercial system on earth. It is described as "Babylon," which for a Jew would evoke the concepts of enslavement and sin. In John's day this term had come to mean a selfish, ungodly way of life that bound people in immoral thought and living. (Rev. 18)

The angel is most likely referring to a great city that those around the globe would know. This city will typify Babylon -- a world center of selfish, evil means for gaining wealth. For a more detailed description of this evil city, read Revelation 17. The angel foretells the great upheaval and destruction soon to fall on the city and its evil enterprises.

The message is a clear call for all to separate themselves from this ungodly way of living, especially God's people. (Rev. 18:4)

Angel Three

The last angel warns against worshipping the image of the beast, or receiving the mark of the beast – actions which will invoke the torments of hell. (vs. 9-10).

I have heard people express the worry that if they someday find themselves in the tribulation, they might accidentally accept the mark of the beast.

So much for that idea. The description of the third angel's message makes clear that anybody who receives the mark of the beast will know exactly what they are doing -- and will know it is in direct disobedience to God's warning.

Antichrist will be powerless to censor these warnings. The three angels will dramatically communicate to millions, visiting every inhabited area on the globe.

Consider the logistics of this angelic mission:

The three angels must proclaim their message to each nation, tribe, and language group. At present our planet has roughly 50,000 cities of 10,000 people or more. If the angels spent just 30 minutes sharing their messages over each of these cities, it would take almost three years to accomplish their task.

Of course, God may have a more streamlined way for the angels to fulfill their assignment; but it is useful for us to consider the sheer magnitude of what is involved. When we reflect on the staggering scale of what Revelation 14 describes, we begin to grasp the Lord's audacity.

Now, we might think that if the whole earth saw enormous angels flying through the skies, proclaiming the truth of the gospel and the doom awaiting the wicked, there would be universal repentance.

Though that seems logical, it isn't human nature.

Notice what Jesus said of his own people after he had come and done great signs before them: "Woe unto thee, Chorazin! Woe unto thee, Bethsaida! For if the mighty works had been done in Tyre and Sidon which were done in you, they would have repented long ago in sackcloth and ashes." (Matt. 11:21)

Sin can so harden hearts that even the most dramatic miracles will not turn them back to God.

Does Anyone Listen?

That brings us to the question, "Are the two witnesses and three angels ultimately successful in their mission?" Yes, praise the Lord. We read John's words in Revelation 15:2 --

> Then I saw what looked like a sea of glass mixed with fire. Those who had conquered [been victorious over] the beast, its image, and the number of its name were standing on the sea of glass holding God's harps in their hands. They sang the song of God's servant Moses and the song of the lamb...

The Holy Spirit caused John to see a throng of people before God's throne who had faced the trial of forced worship of the "image of the beast," and the demand to have the "mark of the beast" placed on them in order to buy and sell (Rev. 13:14-18), and had come through in faith. By God's strength they had resisted Satan's pressure. They heeded the angelic warning, the testimony of the two witnesses, and ministry of the world church. They remained faithful in looking to Jesus to be their savior.

We recognize two things from this amazing story: Satan's fiercest resistance will not prevent the great harvest. God is going to trump Satan's crushing persecution with his audacious supernatural witness.

Can you imagine a Christian walking among the listening crowds as they gaze up at the angels, asking "Excuse me, does anyone want to pray with me to receive Christ?" Remember, so long as anyone can receive Jesus Christ as savior and receive the Holy Spirit into their heart, the church will endure on earth. God will be reaching out to the lost until the last moment.

God will not abandon these new converts, who will desperately need the church community for strength and discipleship in the most difficult of times.

REVIEW OF CHAPTER ELEVEN

1. The three gospel angels are one of God's most extraordinary expressions of audacious love to a lost world. Antichrist may try to keep their appearances off TV, but they will be seen – and heard. Only the most hard-hearted sinners will reject this final appeal to receive Jesus Christ as savior.

2. The Apostle John shows plainly that many will be converted by the dramatic impact of the two witnesses and the three angels. But we must appreciate that, behind the scenes, God will be planting churches, raising up pastors, and sending apostles, prophets, teachers, and evangelists to disciple the multitude of new converts. Today we should be encouraging a bold, expectant faith in future victories. The church will face a great test of endurance, but it will also rise to the peak of its greatest earthly glory, and brightest reflection of Jesus Christ.

CHAPTER TWELVE

Time for Audacious Faith

The woman and her husband had come seeking prayer for healing. As we saw her enter the room - in a wheelchair - my faith wavered. She began explaining how she had lost so much strength in her legs that she could hardly stand any more. But she had heard that we prayed for the sick, and that God heals. So, here she was.

She looked nervous. I *felt* nervous.

Our prayer team looked to the Lord, as we always did. Then we prayed for her, not sure what to expect.

I heard in my heart, "Have her stand up and walk around."

It was an audacious command.

I struggled with my response. How emotionally crushing would it be if she tried to stand, but simply collapsed back into the wheelchair? What would that do to her faith? To *my* faith?

Then, drawing a deep breath, I decided to obey.

I asked her if she would stand up to see what God had done in response to our prayer. She looked doubtful. I said, "Take your time."

She hesitated. Finally she said, "Okay." Slowly she started to rise from the wheelchair. A surprised look came to her face. She kept rising. Then she was standing. She began to walk around the room. Then she started clapping her hands and praising God!

I asked if she wanted to sit back down and rest.

"No, no!" she exclaimed. "What I want is to push this wheelchair straight out of this room and back to my car!"

We watched in joyful amazement as the couple left, side by side, with the woman pushing the wheelchair that had carried her in.

Praise God, indeed. He rewarded her faith, and he rewarded our faith – in all its audacity.

Three Kinds Of Faith

Let me challenge each of us to consider the condition of our faith. If God is ready to respond to audacious faith, do we have it? We must be intentional about growing our faith – and recognize that we need God's help. This is plainly modeled for us in Luke 17:5, in the disciples' prayer: "Lord, increase our faith."

Jesus actually talked about three kinds of faith: "no faith," "little faith," and "great faith."

1. No Faith

Early in Jesus' ministry, the disciples found themselves caught in the middle of a terrible storm on the Sea of Galilee. Despairing for their lives, they woke Jesus -- who was calmly sleeping in the back of their tossing boat. "Master, don't you care that we're perishing?" they cried.

Jesus got up, rebuked the storm, the wind ceased, and the sea went flat. He turned to the open-mouthed disciples and asked, "Do you still have no faith?" (Mk. 4:40)

Most of us might be upset by Jesus' question. "Well, what do you expect?" we probably would protest. "We aren't God! We can't control the weather!"

Wrong answer.

Jesus expected his disciples by now to have gotten the message that God was ready to do impossible things through his ministry. He also expected them to trust that if he was asleep in the boat, then the situation wasn't as dire as they thought.

Most likely the disciples had looked to the four seasoned fishermen among their number for guidance. But when things got out of hand, everyone panicked.

Too often, all of us have tried to handle life by looking to man and not to God.

Notice that the disciples woke Jesus for the express purpose of getting him to share in their alarm: What was he doing sleeping through this calamity, anyway? Sometimes we think God simply isn't keeping up on our current situation.

This story might have had a different ending if the disciples had gone to Jesus earlier, asking him how to handle the choppy seas. Too many times we, as believers, have Jesus in our hearts – yet keep trying to work things out in our own strength and understanding. And when we reach our limits, we panic. The Apostle James declared, "Faith without works is dead [worthless]." (Jam. 2:20) You can't claim to have faith in God, then display none whatsoever when the chips are down.

In the midst of the storm there was no "demonstration of faith" on the part of the disciples, except to take their distress to Jesus. For that moment, they were no different than the unbelieving crowds that continually surrounded him.

Likewise, fear and unbelief frequently move the church to submit to circumstances -- rather than submitting circumstances to God's will.

2. Little Faith

In Matthew's gospel we find many references to "little faith," all associated with the disciples' weak attempts at trusting God's word.

A familiar example is in Matt. 14:29-33 when, during another storm on the Sea of Galilee, Peter sees Jesus walking on the water. "Lord, if that's you," Peter calls, "command me to come to you!"

Jesus answers, "Come!" Peter steps out of the boat and begins walking toward Jesus. But quickly he becomes conscious of the surrounding wind and waves, and starts to sink – shouting in fright for Jesus to rescue him.

As Jesus grabs Peter's flailing hand, he describes Peter's faith as "little."

Frankly, in all history only two people have ever walked on water: Jesus, and Peter. No other disciples followed Peter out of the boat and onto the Sea of Galilee.

Peter shows us that even *little* faith in God's word can be enough to move us into accomplishing impossible things -- if only for a moment.

The lesson here is Peter's choice of focus. When he kept his focus on Jesus, he was capable of defying physics. But as soon as his focus shifted to the wind and waves, and his natural understanding that people do not walk on water, he began to sink.

We need to be aware of our focus – choosing to place it on God's word and on the leading of the Holy Spirit. Only then, by practicing "little faith," can we move ahead toward "great faith."

If instead we choose to stay in the boat and never risk stepping out on God's promises, we will remain stuck in unbelief.

3. Great Faith

Only a few times in Jesus' earthly ministry was he stunned by the degree of someone's faith.

One such incident is recorded in the opening verses of Luke 7. A ranking Roman army officer, concerned about a valued but gravely ill slave, hears of Jesus. Aware of Jewish rules about the separation between Jews and Gentiles, he does not approach Jesus himself but instead sends some Jewish elders with a request: Please come to heal my slave.

The elders implore Jesus to respond, emphasizing that the Roman centurion is a friend of the Jewish people, and helped build their synagogue. Jesus goes with them.

Before they reach the centurion's house, however, they are met by a second delegation – friends of the officer, with another message:

> Lord, do not trouble yourself, for I am not worthy to have you come under my roof; therefore I did not presume to come to you. But only speak the word, and let my servant be healed. For I also am a man set under authority, with soldiers under me; and I say to one, "Go," and he goes, and to another, "Come," and he comes, and to my slave, "Do this," and the slave does it." (Lk. 7:8-6)

At this, the Son of God stops in amazement. Then he turns to the surrounding crowd and says, "I tell you, not even in Israel have I found such great faith!"

Sure enough, when the centurion's friends return to the house, they find the slave completely healed.

The Roman officer understood how the "chain of command" worked. He was not looking at the circumstances of his servant's failing health, but at the authority Jesus had from God. He was convinced that if Jesus commanded divine power to heal, that command would be followed without question.

He had great faith.

Faith Explained

I like the way the Contemporary English Version of the Bible explains faith as taught in the book of Hebrews.

> Faith makes us sure of what we hope for and
> gives us proof of what we cannot see. (Heb
> 11:1)

Biblical faith is always about focusing on God's promises and truth. It grows from finding God's word trustworthy.

Let me give you an example. Imagine that God says to me, "I will give you a better job than the one you lost." God has spoken something into my heart. As I recognize God's voice I must respond to his promise.

I verbalize that promise and say, "God has told me that I am going to get a better job!" My faith makes me "sure" of what I am hoping for – giving it "substance," or reality in my understanding.

The word "hope" in verse 1 of Hebrews 11 points to what we are "trusting God for." Such faith makes me a witness that what God has promised will come to pass, and will eventually be manifested for all to see.

Now, if God has indeed spoken to me, it isn't my responsibility to make the new job happen. It is God's responsibility to fulfill his word. For sure, I need to go out and look for a job; but as I do, I know that God is guiding my steps. My better Job is a fact – even if it is not yet seen.

In his letter to the Romans, Paul cites an Old Testament illustration of great faith: the patriarch Abraham, who believed that even at his advanced age, God would allow him to father a child.

> ...as the scripture says, "I have made you
> father of many nations." So the promise is good

133

in the sight of God .... Abraham believed and hoped, even when there was no reason for hoping, and so became "the father of many nations." Just as the scripture says, "Your descendants will be as many as the stars." He was then almost one hundred years old; but his faith did not weaken when he thought of his body, which was already practically dead, or of the fact that Sarah could not have children. His faith did not leave him, and he did not doubt God's promise; his faith filled him with power, and he gave praise to God. He was absolutely sure that God would be able to do what he had promised. That is why Abraham, through faith, "was accepted as righteous by God." (Rom. 4:17-22 GNB)

Abraham had learned not to look at his impossible circumstances. Instead, he focused on God's promise and trustworthy character. Through a maturing process, Abraham came to believe that the God of life could give the dead womb of Sarah the ability to conceive a baby. From that point on, nothing could shake Abraham's faith. Isaac was a "fact" in Abraham's heart before he was born.

This is the kind of faith that pleases God. (Heb. 11:6)

As we move towards the end times, we must challenge ourselves to have "great faith." God is going to give us impossible assignments to help usher in the great harvest. He will be ready to answer outlandish prayers to help us fulfill our mission.

God alone receives glory when we achieve things beyond our own abilities through his power and strength.

Ditch Diggers Fellowship

In the 1980s, while studying at Fuller Seminary in southern California, I became aware of a Christian organization in England called the "Ditch Diggers Fellowship." It was a group of Christian leaders who had committed themselves to plant churches, preparing for an expected outpouring of the Holy Spirit. They were believing that the Holy Spirit was about to sweep a flood of new believers into the church.

The Ditch Diggers took their name from a story found in 2 Kings 3:16-17.

In that passage we read of three armies traveling through the desert of Edom: the armies of Edom, Israel, and Judah. They ran out of water and found themselves in serious trouble.

They approached the prophet Elisha to pray to God for them so that their forces wouldn't die of thirst. God answered Elisha's prayer, instructing him to have the kings of Edom, Israel, and Judah order their men out into the desert to dig ditches all around their encampment.

It seemed like a crazy idea to the three kings, but they obeyed. God thereupon sent a flash flood, rescuing the armies with the water that filled the ditches.

This group of English Christian leaders adopted this biblical story as a strategy of preparing, by faith, to receive God's coming visitation. They began training pastors, forming new churches, and preparing existing churches to be ready for the coming spiritual harvest.

The image of that faith-filled strategy has never left me.

Digging Faith Ditches

Let's say you accept that God is ready to send a great harvest wave across the world. You humble your heart and say, "Lord how do you want me to prepare for this coming wave?"

As you pray and wait on the Lord, you find God bringing back a long-held desire: You have had a burden to reach schoolchildren for Christ. You recognize that God is in this desire, and you determine to act on it.

Next, a strong impression comes to you to establish 100 after-school homework and Bible study programs in the grammar schools of your county.

Would your level of faith respond with, "Please Lord, I want to do something, but that impression is too much -- it's beyond me"?

That would be a "no faith" response.

A growing-faith response would be, "Lord this seems beyond my ability; but I believe I can do it, because you will help me."

From what we have covered, we already know God wants to be audacious, and is looking for audacious faith in his people. From a step of growing faith, you would move into an opportunity to exercise great faith.

It is scary to launch into something that may seem beyond your abilities, but that is part of true faith. Even failure is part of growing towards great faith.

How would great faith possibly look in response to the illustration I just set up for you?

Let's say you organize a prayer group to cover you and your efforts to reach into the local grammar schools. Then you begin identifying 100 schools in your city, and survey them for a willingness to allow after-school homework and Bible programs. You ask God to give you a plan and help you calculate the costs for doing such programs.

Then, in faith, you make a list of businesses and churches to approach about funds to support the programs. You also stay alert for people to join the leadership team you expect that God will provide to help you.

When disappointment comes or opposition arises, you stay in prayer and keep confessing God's will. You may have people say that you have set an impossible goal, but you remember that God almost always gives us assignments beyond what we can do -- so that he gets the glory.

I believe God is ready to hand out city- and nation-changing assignments. But he must have a people who believe we can accomplish whatever he wants us to do.

When the flood comes, it is too late to "dig ditches." We have to exercise our faith now.

Do you sense that there may be far more God wants to do through your life? Ask him to show you what it is. Then be prepared to respond and grow in your faith to do what he is leading you do.

REVIEW OF CHAPTER TWELVE

1. God is going to become more audacious in his witness as we move towards the last days. We must match God's audacity with faith that will allow God to greatly use us.

2. The church must move from little faith to great faith! God is ready to reach whole nations. Now is the time to refuse to see any limits on what God can do. Growing faith does not always see how to accomplish what God is asking -- but it does act on the little it has been given.

3. Building great faith is part of the church's need to get ready. Like England's "Ditch Diggers Fellowship," we must begin audaciously creating spiritual "ditches" (churches, schools, ministries, organizations) to receive the ripe harvest that God sends to be pastored and discipled.

CHAPTER THIRTEEN

It's Later Than You Think!

Have you ever been on a long family car trip with the kids in the back seat asking incessantly, "How much longer until we get there?"

Similarly, the church is on a long journey -- and its leadership is constantly asked, "How much longer until Jesus comes back?"

Once my children were old enough to read, I used to tell them: "Do you see that sign up ahead? It says our destination is a certain number of miles away from where we are now." This actually got my children quieted down and peering ahead for mileage signs, trying to spot them before my wife and I did.

Jesus knew the church was in for a long journey, so he gave it prophetic signs to help it gauge its distance from the final destination. Those signs are in our Bible – and we should not fail to use them.

In growing up, I used to hear preachers say, "Jesus might come back any day now, so we must be ready!" I'm afraid that is tantamount to telling kids in the car, "We'll be there any minute, so just hang on." Parents know better than to do this. The children quickly get impatient and the questioning starts all over again.

Jesus won't come back until we have gone past the signs he posted on our spiritual highway. We have to use the divine signs to get any sense of how near we are to the end this age.

Signs That Have Already Come To Pass

Some of the signs have disappeared from our rear view mirror. Others we can see through the windshield.

The Destruction Of Jerusalem in 70 A.D.

In Matthew 24, Mark 13, and Luke 21 Jesus predicted the destruction of the Herodian Temple. That took place in 70 A.D. about 40 years after Jesus' death. It was the first marker Jesus gave his disciples to prepare them for the end of the age.[xiv]

The Restored Fig Tree

The second sign that has already passed is one we discussed in Chapter 3: the "restored fig tree." This sign speaks of the restoration of the nation of Israel and its capital. [xv] (Matt. 24:32; Mk. 13:28-29, Lk. 21:29-30) This is an essential sign, because many of Jesus' and the apostles' predictions are based on the political existence of the Jewish nation.

Israel Will Be A "Burdensome Stone" For The Nations

Another sign we don't need to look hard for is Israel becoming a problem for surrounding nations, stirring up conflict.

> Behold, I will make Jerusalem a cup of trembling to all the peoples all around .... And in that day I will make Jerusalem a burdensome stone for all peoples. All who lift it shall be slashed (injured), and all the nations of the earth will be gathered against it. (Zech.12:2-3)

Notice that the signs extend from the time of the early church right into contemporary history. Shouldn't the fact that we are passing important markers make us look to our readiness?

Signs Yet To Come

Here are five key signs we as Christian leaders should be preparing the church to recognize in our spiritual journey to the end of this age.

1. The Jewish temple will be reconstructed in Jerusalem at some point, because it is the one Antichrist will desecrate. It is not a temple God wants built, but it is a temple the Jews will build. (Matt. 24:15; Mk. 13:14; 2 Thess. 2:3-4)

2. The great rebellion, or falling away from the church. This will be so noticeable that Paul says it will be a clear sign to an alert church. (2 Thess. 2:3) The hallmark of this rebellion will be outright rejection of sound doctrinal truth, and a love for ear-tickling spiritual lies. (2 Thess. 2:10-11; 2 Tim. 4:3-4)

3. The revealing of the Antichrist, or man of sin ("Lawlessness"). Again, this will be so evident that the church will recognize this evil leader for who he is. Paul says he will work false signs and wonders that will deceive the lost. (2 Thess. 2:3, 9-10)

4. The gospel will be preached to every "ethnos" (people group). (Matt. 24:14; Mk. 13:10) The late missionary and researcher/editor for Frontier Missions, Dr. Ralph Winters, declared that the reaching of the last "unreached" people groups by the middle of this century is quite feasible. [xvi] Dr.

Winters stated categorically that we are close to finishing the great commission.

5. The "first fruits" harvest wave among the Jewish People. (Rev.14:4b; Romans 11:25)

Besides these five signposts are two enormous ones we have already explored: The arrivals of the Two Witnesses and the three Gospel Angels.

This doesn't constitute an exhaustive list of last-days signs, but it certainly lets us see how the Lord wants the church to mark our advance toward his coming again.

How Do We Prepare God's People?

"Get ready, get ready," sounds the drumbeat. But how? Let me suggest from scripture ways that spiritual leaders can prepare God's people as we move forward.

1. Start Telling The Truth

Scripture is clear: A generation of the church will face harsh realities at the very end of time. We need to stop preaching "escapism" that builds false hopes. We need instead to build courage to face with grace what so much of the third-world church is already facing.

Yet in this harsh suffering of the end-time church will come the most awesome expression of God's glory on earth. Let's tell the truth that best prepares believers.

2. Focus On Faith, Not Fear

The Lord wants his church to face the close of this age with faith, not with fear. Three times Jesus tells his disciples, "Don't be troubled [frightened or alarmed]." (Matt. 24:6; Mk. 13:7; Lk. 21:9) The Lord wants us to recognize he is fully aware of what is coming -- and he is in control. The enemy may look strong; but stronger is he who is in us than he who is in the world. (1 Jn. 4:4)

3. Stay Awake (Renewed And Ready)

Jesus repeatedly called his church to be alert -- on guard and watching unto prayer. (Mk. 13:23; Lk. 21:36) To keep God's people spiritually alert and on guard means leaders and teachers must continuously work at spiritual renewal. We must not be distracted, or careless. It is a time to stay focused on God's word and listen to the Holy Spirit's leading each day. The Lord specifically promised us he would be with us through it all. (Matt. 28:20; Mk.1 6:20)

4. Expect Supernatural Support

We must not only focus on faith but on God's amazing grace. Remember, grace is unearned strength and power that God gives to his people. In Jesus' great commission in the Gospel of Mark, he made it clear that he would not only be with us but would supernaturally help us.

> Then his disciples went out and preached everywhere, while the Lord kept working with them and confirming the message by the signs that accompanied it. (Mk. 16:20)

I have had church members and Bible students ask me how the church will survive the time of Antichrist if we have to accept the mark of beast to buy and sell food. (Rev. 13:17)

I tell them that Jesus remains our example in all things. Do we imagine he turned water to wine, multiplied a few loaves and fishes to feed thousands, walked on water and calmed a storm to just give us "wow" stories about himself?

No. He was declaring that with God, "nothing is impossible." (Lk. 1:37) Through audacious faith we will find him to be our provider, healer, and encourager, no matter what we have to face. The end-times church will be "naturally supernatural."

5. Use God's Wisdom To Escape Danger

There is also a practical reason why we need to be instructing God's people on end-times signs. They must understand what is coming so they know how to respond to the dangers.

In the gospel of Luke, the evangelist records Jesus warning his disciples to "watch and pray" so they might escape things that were coming. (Lk. 21:36) We have already shown that there will be a generation of the church that will face the tribulation.

Consequently Jesus is not teaching in Luke 21 a hope of escaping the harsh trials ahead for the church. Jesus' reference to "escaping" in this passage is dealing with common sense.

The goal of the Lord is not for us to suffer, but to be a witness no matter the cost. If we can avoid pointless suffering or persecution, we should do so.

For example, Jesus warned the early church of the coming destruction of Jerusalem with the command to "flee to the mountains" as they saw that time arriving. (Matt. 24:16) I have already told the story of how the Jerusalem church in 70 A.D. is reported to have walked out of Jerusalem before the Roman armies marched up to surround and destroy it. Jesus also told his disciples that when persecution came they should "flee to other places." (Matt. 10:23)

Please don't misunderstand me. I am not advocating buying food, ammunition, and holing up in a cabin in the mountains, hiding from the government. Rather, I am advocating giving God's people enough understanding to be discerning in the days ahead.

Jesus told his disciples that he was "sending them as sheep among wolves." They were then to be "wise as serpents and harmless as doves." (Matt. 10:16) We are to be alert to avoid unnecessary danger -- but we are never to inflict harm on anyone in the process.

An Honest Assessment

We are living in a generation that has seen two very important signs come to pass: Israel restored as a nation, and national Israel becoming a flashpoint of world conflict.

We are seeing a third benchmark reached: the gospel penetrating to every people group on the planet. It might happen sooner than later, but it is closer than most think. God is the one who will decide how "deep" we have to go to consider a people group reached by the gospel.

The rest of the prophetic signs remaining to be fulfilled could easily happen within 10 years of Antichrist stepping onto the world stage. (2 Thess 2:3) And only God can decide when to initiate that decade of the final signs.

I have said we are within a generation or two of the last days being fulfilled. Perhaps there are more generations to come, but I doubt it. The Apostle Peter teaches that God is holding back on his coming because of his love for the lost -- so none should perish. (2 Peter 3:9) How long will he hold back? We don't know, because his love is unfathomable. But we do know what he has told us to watch for.

We have seen the estimate that by the year 2045 the world population will be at 9 billion people. That estimate assumes 6 billion will be non-Christian. The year 2045 is only 30 years away: Time is short and the task is great.

This is why God is going to become audacious in his support of the gospel. Speculating about timing is a distraction the devil would love to have us veer into. Meanwhile, God is ready to move. The nations are being shaken. The final harvest is ripe.

We must get ready!

REVIEW OF CHAPTER THIRTEEN

1. The church must refocus on the "signs of the times" that the Lord provided. The purpose of prophetic signs is to allow the church to track its position on its journey through this age. The main point of teaching the signs is to give the church hope -- and a sense of urgency --to prepare for the end times.

2. Jesus has given clear instructions not only on how to recognize the times we are in, but on how to prepare for what is coming. It is a poor spiritual leader who ignores this clear biblical emphasis on keeping the church alert and ready.

3. We cannot be dogmatic about when Jesus will return, or exactly how the events of the last days will unfold. But with Jesus' signs already coming to pass, it would be wrong to think we have unlimited time. The church has a huge task ahead in reaching the rest of the unsaved in the world. Above all, God is ready to become audacious in supporting the gospel through willing, prepared believers.

A Net-breaking Harvest

Peter sat in his fishing boat listening to the popular rabbi teaching a large crowd on the beach. Peter was tired and discouraged: He had worked all night and caught nothing.

The rabbi had asked Peter if he could use the boat to teach from, so he would have space to address the people crowded around. Finally the rabbi finished and dismissed the crowd.

Somehow this rabbi sensed Peter's discouragement. He told Peter to take the boat out into the deeper water and let down his nets again.

Peter was surprised. He guessed that the teacher wanted to help, but he explained that they had tried all night -- so it would be useless to try any more fishing that day.

Still, there was something about this man. Against his better judgment, Peter found himself saying, "At your word, I will go let down the nets."

No sooner had they reached deep water and cast out their nets than there came a huge pull on the lines. The boat began to heel dangerously close to the water as fish filled the net.

Amazed and excited, Peter and his crew began hauling on the lines -- but there were so many fish the net began to break. The boat started to take on water.

Peter yelled to his fishing partners John and James to bring their boat and help him gather in these fish. As the second boat drew alongside and dropped its net, it too filled up and began to sink under the weight of such a huge catch.

Peter knew this was not a natural event. He was immediately overwhelmed by his unworthiness to be in the presence of a rabbi who against all likelihood could call forth a net-breaking haul of fish. At that moment, Jesus called Peter to come follow him – promising he would make Peter a "fisher of men."

Jesus wanted to make a supernatural point with these fishermen. He was calling them to leave their fishing business and join him in drawing people into the net of the Kingdom of God. (Lk. 5:10) And this harvest of people would be "net breaking."

God is shaking the nations one last time to produce a vast harvest. The divine seismic work began with the first coming of Christ. It has been building throughout the present age.

We may have been working hard for the Lord, yet catching few people into the Kingdom. But things are about to change.

Now we need to launch into the deep to let down "nets" made of every church, denomination, and Christian organization. Such a commitment will take great faith. The key is that we are doing it "at his word."

In truth the church isn't ready for the harvest tsunami that God is building. But he is not going to let this situation continue. He has no plan B. The Lord is going to bring in this worldwide harvest through his church.

Now is the time to dream impossible dreams for the glory of God. Now is the time to get ready.

The Coming Books of this Series

In Book Two we will look closely at the condition of the church and outline the need for both personal revival and corporate reformation. We will also trace waves of revival throughout church history, seeing how God always has been faithful to renew and restore the church.

This review will give us confidence to look for the last great outpouring of God's Spirit, which will inspire and empower the church for the days ahead. God is ready to form a church so full of his glory that the nations will be drawn to it. (Isa. 60:1-2)

In Book Three, concluding the series, we will look at exciting new strategies for planting churches and building life-changing discipleship. The emphasis will be on the patterns Jesus laid out for doing church, doing discipleship, and completing the great commission.

We also will squarely face the last great enemy of the church: disunity. If we are to surf the harvest tsunami that the Lord is going to release, all of God's churches must come together.

It means we must agree on what is "essential unity," built around the goal of the Great Commission. We do not have to agree on every point of doctrine, but we do have to agree on who Jesus is, and on his commission to the church.

Only with all churches, denominations, and Christian organizations united – each providing unique visions and abilities -- will we have the capacity to disciple such a staggering harvest.

I believe the latter rain of God's Spirit is beginning to fall, inspiring a new generation to live a Word-based, Spirit-empowered life.

Are you sensing that rain? My prayer is that you will join those who are already preparing for this extraordinary, history-capping chapter of the church.

It is worth saying again: God will use whomever makes themselves ready.

APPENDIX I

The Hundred and Forty-four Thousand
(The saving of Israel)

The Book of Revelation's seventh chapter depicts 144,000 Jewish people who are saved in the last days. (Rev. 7:4-8) Some readers see this passage as describing a special salvation for a super-spiritual group of Jewish Christians after the church has been raptured.

Such is not the case. Remember, so long as the gospel is being preached, and people are being saved and receiving the Holy Spirit, the church remains on earth. This passage is simply the Apostle John speaking to the future fulfillment of what the Apostle Paul believed God for, concerning the nation of Israel:

> And they also, if they continue not in their unbelief, shall be grafted in: for God is able to graft them in again. For if you (gentiles) were cut out of that which is by nature a wild olive tree, and were grafted contrary to nature into a good olive tree; how much more shall these, which are the natural branches, be grafted into their own olive tree? For I would not, brethren, have you ignorant of this mystery, lest you be wise in your own conceits, that a hardening in part has befallen Israel, until the fullness of the Gentiles be come in; and so all Israel shall be saved: even as it is written, There shall come out of Zion the Deliverer; He shall turn away ungodliness from Jacob...." (Romans 11:23-26)

What we see in the beginning of Revelation 7 is that God is withholding judgment of the wicked until the salvation of the "first fruits" of Israel occurs. (Rev. 14:4b) Remember that the "first fruits" of a harvest were offered to God in thanksgiving for the whole. The first-fruits offering caused the entire harvest to be blessed by God.

Through John, the Spirit is speaking here of the beginning of Israel's return to the Lord. The first fruits are taken equally from every tribe, representing that the whole nation is being blessed and made acceptable to God. According to Zechariah, all Israel will be converted on the very day the Lord Jesus returns (Zechariah 12; see also Romans 11:26).

Revelation 7 further depicts a "sealing" of these Jewish believers. God's name is placed on their foreheads as protection from any judgment coming on the wicked. But such a sealing is the same thing that happens to every born-again believer. (Eph.1:13 and Rev. 22:4)

Paul is clear that no true believer is destined to share God's wrath against the wicked. (1 Thess. 5:9) John is simply pointing out that these Jews, like Israel in ancient Egypt, are to be sheltered by God from the judgments he will pour out. (Ex. 8:22; 9:26)

In Revelation 14: 4, John declares that these Jewish converts will live "pure chaste lives" (which does not exclude honorable marriage). The phrase that these 144,000 "follow the Lamb [Jesus] wherever he goes" refers to their commitment to a "Christ-like living," and zeal to follow his will. (Rev. 14:4b) This should be the testimony of every born-again believer. (Rom. 8:29)

These first-fruits Jews will be able to sing their own unique "song of redemption" that only the saved can sing. Scripture is clear that all God's people will sing a new song of redemption. The twenty-four elders who represent the complete church (both Old and New Testaments) will sing a new song before the throne of God. (Rev. 5: 9) We will each have our unique song of salvation.

What we see in Rev. 7:1-8 and Rev.14:1-5 is God beginning to redeem Israel and re-graft the nation into salvation history. The first-fruits Jewish believers will be used to advance the gospel, along with the rest of the end-times church.

The Number 144,000 is Figurative

The number "twelve" features prominently in the passage about the 144,000 Jewish witnesses. We read there are 12,000 Jews saved from the 12 tribes of Israel. This expression of twelve needs to be seen as a representative number.

For example, in Revelation 21 there are the 12 apostles representing the whole church as the 12 foundations of the heavenly city's walls (Rev. 21:14); and the 12 tribes representing all of Israel as the 12 gates to the new heavenly city. (Rev. 21:12) The 24 elders in Rev. 4:4 represent the combining of the church and Israel as the full, complete people of God reigning with Christ.

So, the reference to 12,000 Jews being saved from each tribe doesn't mean that God has a quota: 12,000 per tribe, and that's it! Rather, the number 12 signifies that a "large number of Jews representing "all" of Israel will be the first fruits as Israel begins returning to God.

Can you imagine the impact of so many Jews being saved worldwide in such a short period of time, with many returning to their nation to witness for Christ?   And remember -- this movement is just the beginning.

It is the answer to Paul's lifelong prayer (Rom. 10:1) with Israel awakening from its spiritual slumber. (Rom. 11:8, 25)

For God's people, fulfillment of this prophecy must become a key prayer target. Like the Prophet Daniel, who began to earnestly pray as he realized the time of Israel's captivity was coming to an end (Daniel 9), so must we pray for the first fruits of Israel to come forth in this epic restoration.

APPENDIX II

The Three Falls of Satan

SATAN'S FIRST FALL

The First Fall of Satan occurred when he corrupted himself and ceased being "Lucifer" -- the anointed cherub who led worship in the third heaven (2 Cor. 12:2) and served at God's throne. In this fall, Satan was cast out of the third heaven -- taking with him about one-third of the angels, who had followed him in rebellion against God. (Ezek. 28:14-16; Isa. 14:12-15; Rev. 12:4)

SATAN'S SECOND FALL

After Adam and Eve sinned, Satan became known as the "ruler of this world." (Jn. 12:31; 14:30; 16:11) He had some measure of authority and power over humanity through the Old Testament era. (Refer back to the beginning of Chapter Three for a more detailed explanation of Satan's authority in the second heaven.)

Jesus in his ministry recognized the fall of Satan from the second heaven. In Luke 10:17, the 70 disciples returned from their mission elated that demonic spirits were subject to them.

Jesus refers to the casting out of demons as the sign that God, through Jesus' ministry and life, has limited Satan's authority to resist -- allowing the church to rob from his house. (Lk. 11:20-21; see also 1 Jn. 3:8) This power over the demonic by the church was the evidence that Satan was being thrown down from the second heaven. The disciples were now able to confront and overthrow his workers.

As Jesus faced crucifixion at the end of his ministry, he stated that the cross signaled Satan being cast down from the position he had enjoyed in the heavens. (Jn. 12:31) And in Ephesians 4:8, we see Jesus in his ascension leading a "triumphal procession" of defeated enemies (Satan and his workers).

In Revelation 12 we see a review of Satan's first two falls. One occurs in Rev. 12:3-5, in which Satan and his angels are thrown out of the upper heavens and take up the battle against Israel and the coming messiah. But then at the Resurrection (the catching up of the child) we see another fall. In Rev. 12:7-9, Satan is said to be cast down to the earth (or the physical heaven), where he carries out his battle with the church.

So, where did Satan fall to? He fell to the atmosphere of this world. Paul refers to Satan as being the "prince of the power of the air." (Eph. 2:2) These are the visible "heavens": those we can see, and fly through.

SATAN'S THIRD AND FINAL FALL

Finally, the Bible teaches that Satan will be defeated once and for all and cast into hell forever after the Millennial reign of Christ. (Rev. 20:10)

APPENDIX III

Editor Rick Wood recently wrote an editorial for the U.S. Center of World Missions magazine *Frontier Ventures*. In this article he described the growing instability of Middle Eastern nations, and pointed out that with the rise of "virtual terror organizations" -- such as ISIS -- that are recruiting and expanding their influence through the internet, the Islamic nations are in crisis.

Wood pointed out that Muslims themselves are struggling to make sense of the recruiting of young Muslims to kill other Muslims, in the name of their religion.

Egyptian President Abdel Fattah al Sisi, in a speech to the Al-Azhar University in Cairo -- the foremost Islamic training center – stated, "...this umma [Muslim world] is being torn, it is being destroyed, it is being lost -- and it is being lost by our own hands..."

Woods ended his editorial saying:

> God is shaking the "house of Islam" and we must be ready and equipped to present to Muslims a loving and culturally sensitive presentation of the "hope that lies within us." More Muslims are coming to Christ now than at any time since Muhammad, and the number of movements to Christ [among Muslims] is growing rapidly.... Let's equip ourselves for the Kingdom breakthroughs in the Muslim world <u>that God is preparing for us</u>."[xvii]
>
> *[Emphasis mine]*

Endnotes

[i] A Double Prophecy: A double prophecy comes when a prophet gives a prophetic message that has two fulfillments. The first fulfillment is a "shadow" of a more distant, deeper, future fulfillment of the prediction. To best identify a double prophecy, we usually need a New Testament writer to recognize the deeper fulfillment. For example, we have the Apostle Peter seeing a deeper meaning in Joel's prophecy of the worldwide outpouring of the Holy Spirit (Acts 2:17). Peter also sees the deeper fulfillment in King David's reference to his death and hope of resurrection (Ps. 16:8-10); the phrase "nor allow your holy one to see corruption" has a deeper fulfillment in Jesus Christ's resurrection. (Acts 2:2-27)

[ii] Ecclesiastical History, tr. C. F. Crusè, 3d ed., in Greek Ecclesiastical Historians, 6 vols. (London: Samuel Bagster and Sons, 1842), p. 110 (3:5). The early Christian scholar Eusebius wrote: "The whole body, however, of the church at Jerusalem, having been commanded by a divine revelation, given to men of approved piety there before the war, removed from the city, and dwelt at a certain town beyond the Jordan, called Pella."[3]

[iii] The Hebrew-Greek Key Study Bible. Gospel of Matthew. (AMG Publishers Chattanooga,TN), 1996, pg.1147

[iv] John Lambert. "Massive Prayer and Missions Movements of the 90's." (July/August, 2014); Vol.36.No.4, p.21

[v] David Taylor. "Intercessory Missions." Mission Frontier. (Juy/August, 2014); Vol.36. No.4, p.4-5

[vi] Ralph Winters. "The Amazing Count Down." Mission Frontier, (September - October, 2009): Vol. 31, No. 5, p.30

[vii] Data taken from a web site called Religious - Tolerance, "Growth rate of Christianity to Islam." Several studies projected Christianity's growth rate at a little better than the world growth rate over the next 40 years. This may be revised depending on how aggressive and successful Christian missions are in the coming decades. The projections are based primarily on birthrates.

[viii] Vinson Synan. In the Latter Days_(Ann Arbor, Michigan: Servant Books), 1983. pg. 5-7

[ix] Robert Costello (Editor in Chief). Random House Webster's College Dictionary. (New York, Random House, 1991)

[x] Jerry Trousdale; Miraculous Movements, Thomas Nelson publisher, Nashville, 2012, pg.133

xi Jerry Trousdale, pg. 24

xii In this story, John is told not to measure the outer court or the court of the Gentiles (vs. 2). John is told that the outer court was to be given to "strangers" (gentiles) who will possess it and rule over it for 42 months. These strangers, according to Dr. Albert Barnes, are false believers who are living a false or compromised faith during this time. [12] They are not to be measured because they are not truly a part of the church, but will eventually be weeded out at Jesus' coming. (Matt. 13:40)

xiii The Prophet Daniel also speaks of this time period. (Daniel 7:25; 12:7)

xiv In truth, there is a double prophecy inside this prediction that speaks to the final destruction of Jerusalem at the very end of this age but this is a discussion not to be dealt with in this book.

xv The restoration of Israel as a nation has signaled the end of the "times of the Gentiles" (Lk. 21:24) According to Jamieson, Fausset, and Brown's Commentary, this is the end of the Gentile political dominance over Jerusalem and the emergence of Israel as a nation once again.

xvi Ralph Winters, "What Are the Resources?", Mission Frontiers, (Sept.-Oct., 2009, vol.31, no.5) p.32

xvii Rick Wood, "New Era," Frontier Ventures, (Mar.- April 2015, vol.37, no.2) p.5